THE RHINELAND MYSTICS

THE RESOURCE ROOM
CHURCH HOUSE
9 THE CLOSE
WINCHESTER
SO23 9LS

D1152269

B44/11

Also published by SPCK

Beguine Spirituality
– an anthology

Edited and introduced by
Fiona Bowie

Translations by
Oliver Davies

THE RHINELAND MYSTICS
An Anthology

Introduced, edited and translated by
Oliver Davies

First published in Great Britain 1989
SPCK
Holy Trinity Church
Marylebone Road
London NW1 4DU

© Oliver Davies 1989

All rights reserved. No part of this book may be reproduced or
transmitted in any form or by any means, electronic or
mechanical, including photocopying, recording, or by any
information storage and retrieval system, without permission in
writing from the publisher.

British Library Cataloguing in Publication Data

The Rhineland mystics: an anthology.
1. Christian life. Mysticism
I. Davies, Oliver
248.2'2

ISBN 0-281-04423-6

Typeset by Rowland Phototypesetting Ltd
Bury St Edmunds, Suffolk
Printed in Great Britain by
the Courier Press Ltd, Tiptree

To Alice,
and the gift of new life

Contents

Preface   ix

PART ONE: INTRODUCTION
The Mysticism of Being   3
Leading Figures   5
'The Ground of the Soul'   16
The Historical Background   17
The Brethren of the Free Spirit   19
A North European School of Mysticism   21

PART TWO: SELECTIONS
Meister Eckhart   27
Johannes Tauler   63
Jan van Ruusbroec   88
The *German Theology*   105
The *Book of Spiritual Poverty*   117

Select Bibliography   127

Preface

This book is the result of a great love for the mysticism of the Rhineland and a conviction that the achievement of these mystical writers deserves not only scholarly evaluation but an accessible introduction to their work for the purposes in particular of personal meditation. There is always a danger that great spiritual writing will be confined to academic circles or will remain trapped in major libraries in obscure languages or in inadequate translations. Some writers have fared better than others in these respects, but all are deserving of a central place in the devotional life of our age. It is my hope that these writers from the medieval Rhineland will feed many, as they have fed me.

Oliver Davies
Mieders, Tyrol
Feast of the Nativity 1988

PART 1

Introduction

The Mysticism of Being

The fourteenth century writings represented in this book constitute one of the greatest flowerings of the mystical spirit in the experience of the Christian Church. This alone would serve to recommend them, but there is an additional reason why these writers enjoy such a special importance for us today. That is the *communicability* of their particular kind of spirituality.

Anyone who has read widely in the field of medieval mysticism will know that a good deal of it only appeals to the specialized tastes of scholars tutored in an idiom of expression and a sensibility which is quite foreign to our modern experience and preferences. We need think only of the emaciated figure of St Bernard of Clairvaux whose physical presence became so abhorrent to his brethren that they requested that he live in separate quarters. A gastric disorder, probably brought on by severe penitential practices, caused him to be sick so frequently that a hole had to be dug for this purpose beside his stall in the choir. We might think also of the young Henry Suso who expressed his deeply felt piety by carving the initials IHS into the flesh of his own chest ('so that the blood flowed copiously'), or of the baroque visions of the saints which were the lot of Elisabeth of Schönau. There is no doubt that in terms of spiritual idiom and practice a good deal of the life of the Middle Ages, and of its greatest saints, seems remote and alien to us, and challenges our modern belief that sanctity must have something to do with psychological and physical 'wholeness'. The presentation of much medieval material to a modern readership therefore requires more than the translation of the words used; it requires an editorial translation of the entire world-view, the literary and spiritual conventions which support and engender it. If we want to penetrate that world in its own reality, then we will need the services of an editor, an interpreter, who can help us discover the deeper and often familiar meanings which lie behind a seemingly alien culture.

What do we mean therefore when we say that, in general, the writings of the fourteenth century Rhineland mystics do *not* require that kind of interpretative exercise? What constitutes their communicability? The answer is to be found first in the kind of mysticism which was theirs as gift and, second, in the terminology which they adapted and developed in order to communicate that gift to others.

The word the Germans use for the mysticism of the Rhineland is *Wesensmystik*, which we may translate as a 'mysticism of essence' or, since we are not so inclined to think in terms of 'essences' today, as a 'mysticism of being'. The meaning is clear: rather than drawing on the spiritual and cultural traditions of their contemporary world for their inspiration, the Rhineland mystics were concerned to penetrate to the deepest, timeless levels of purely *inward* experience. They knew God in the inner recesses of the human soul, as a Presence, as an infinitely transcendent potentiality. Above all, they conceived of the commerce between God and his human creatures in *existential* terms, and they explored the paths of mystical knowledge in a language that was spare, effective and philosophically grounded. It is with regard to the latter point, of course, that they were closest to their age, for much of the terminology of Eckhart and Tauler, Ruusbroec, the *German Theology* and the *Book of Spiritual Poverty* owes a good deal to the philosophical discussions of the late Middle Ages. And yet it seems that that particular way of talking about mystical experience has over the centuries worn exceptionally well: 'superessential', 'detachment', 'ground of the soul', 'nothingness', 'ceasing to become'. Other of their characteristic phrases derive from earlier texts (biblical, patristic and medieval) and reflect a union of tradition with the poetic imagination: e.g. 'spiritual poverty' (Matt 5.3) 'birth of God in the soul' (Origen, St Gregory of Nyssa), 'the touch of God' (St Gregory the Great).

The Rhineland mystics were, of course, creatures of their own age (as are we all), and yet we almost feel that their clear-headed and telling accounts of the spiritual journey communicate to us today as easily as they did to their own contemporaries. After all, our own age is one which has seen the rise of two important philosophical movements, phenomenology and existentialism, both of which have sought to get away from what is most culturally conditioned and to come to grips with what is always and everywhere the same: the inner structures of human consciousness. It is perhaps not surprising therefore that at least two modern philosophers (Martin Heidegger and Stanislas Breton) know and refer to the work of Meister Eckhart. To this extent we can perhaps say that we have a special sensitivity to the voice of the Rhineland mystics, although it comes to us across a gap of over six hundred years. It may be also that we have a special need for their message, which is one of a deeply-felt dependency on God and of a capacity to inhabit our own 'innermost place' where we enter a state of profound union with him. The formal and ritualistic side of religion has been seriously questioned in recent years; the religiously-minded demand, rightly, an element of personal experience in their relationship with God. And it is in the context of this, a widespread search for what is most *essential* to religion, the sense of a real 'indwelling' of ourselves in God and of God in us, that these mystics and texts have most to offer us.

Leading Figures

MEISTER ECKHART

Although I will reserve the biographical background of our mystics for a later section, it would be as well to say something at this point about the leading personalities of the movement, and to give a sense of the evolution of the Rhineland school, which, to all intents and purposes, begins with the towering figure of Meister Eckhart.

Following the papal condemnation in 1329 of twenty-eight

propositions taken from his work, Meister Eckhart fell into almost total obscurity. When in 1575 the Jesuit movement in Spain placed the works of Tauler and Ruusbroec on their own index of prohibited books (largely as a defensive manoeuvre in their contest with the Dominicans), there was no mention of Meister Eckhart, whose name presumably was judged to be wholly innocuous and of purely historical interest, if it was known at all. Indeed, it was not until the Viennese scholar Franz Pfeiffer published selections from the German works of Meister Eckhart in 1855 that the cultural world at large became aware of the existence of the 'Eckhartian way'. Eckhart quickly came to occupy a unique, if much disputed, position in European cultural history; Hegel claimed him for the cause of Idealism while Nietzsche and Schopenhauer make respectful mention of him (as in the present century Martin Heidegger has identified him as a precursor of his own philosophy of Being). During the second half of the nineteenth century Protestant and Catholic scholars each sought to claim Eckhart for their respective camps, as his own distinctive, highly original, philosophical system emerged.

Two vital points have resulted from the progress of Eckhart scholarship. The first is that Meister Eckhart enjoyed enormously high status as a thinker and teacher during his own lifetime. He was twice sent to Paris to represent his own Dominican Order at the Dominican chair of philosophy there, an honour which he shares with St Thomas Aquinas alone. Second, it is now known that Meister Eckhart was neither a deviant (or even bad) Thomist, nor did he spontaneously generate; recent research in particular has shown that Eckhart belonged to a Dominican school of radical, late Augustinianism. Eckhart therefore stands within a tradition, albeit one which was obscured to posterity by the triumphant rise of the alternative Dominican school of Thomism. The retrieval of Eckhart's origins, and our better grasp today of his place in the evolution of scholastic thought, has deepened our understanding of his message and clarified his position as one of the seminal mystical theologians of the Christian tradition.

Meister Eckhart's entire system, extending over a wide range of Latin and German texts, can be summed up as the attempt to expound in terms of an advanced metaphysics the profoundly God-centred experience of the highest mystical union. Eckhart is, and never ceases to be, a *mystical* theologian. This is the key to our understanding of his work. Whereas the discourse of theology and that of mysticism (which tips towards the poetic) are generally kept strictly apart, in Eckhart they come together. Thus, whereas mystics such as Walter Hilton, St Teresa of Avila and St John of the Cross, speaking from the heart of mystical experience, proclaim their 'nothingness' in the face of the Creator, Meister Eckhart constructs an entire ontology, or philosophy of Being, around the principle that all that exists lacks substantial essence: 'God alone truly exists'[1] and the creature is 'pure nothingness'.[2] A second element emerges at this stage, which is also a result of its experiential grounding: the dynamic character of his thinking. This leads to apparent inconsistencies which, in reality, are simply the deepening of his thought, its gathering momentum, as Eckhart's mind penetrates further into the realities he is exploring. Thus the original starting point for his ontology was the view that we *possess* Being whereas God *is* Being. From this, as we have seen, he progressed to the view that only God truly exists, and the final stage is reached when Eckhart defines God as *puritas essendi*, the 'purity' or 'essence' of Being.[3] If God is the cause of *Being*, Eckhart argues, then he cannot be Being itself; rather he must transcend Being. And so the true nature of God finally becomes *intelligere* ('to think', 'to know', or, 'to understand'), for understanding or knowledge, with the unity that this implies, is the ultimate primacy.

The nature of God then for Eckhart is rationality in the sense of self-understanding and self-knowing: 'Intellect is the temple of God. Nowhere does God dwell more truly than in His temple . . . God is intellect which lives in knowledge of itself alone'.[4] But what of man, made in God's image? If the nature of God is rationality, then rationality, too, is our own essential nature, since we were created in his image. And this is what Eckhart believes. Our rational nature is not only God-given; it is an immediate reflection of the Divine Nature itself. It participates mysteriously and essentially in the self-reflexive activity of the Godhead. Of course, when Eckhart speaks of 'intellect', he does not mean that faculty which allows us to work out sums or read difficult books; he means rather our own self-reflexive nature as conscious beings, our capacity to understand, to be aware: consciousness itself. The root, or source, of that consciousness Eckhart calls the 'ground of the soul', and it is to that innermost space that we must retreat from the world and its images. There human consciousness transcends itself and participates directly in the activity of the Divine Intellect, a unitive process which Eckhart calls the 'birth of God in the soul'.

This potentiality for self-transcendence and union with the Divine Mind which resides within human consciousness Eckhart calls the 'spark of the soul', and it becomes the point of orientation for the spiritual journey which is both a journey within, into our innermost essence, and a journey into the Other, who is God. The manner of this journey in terms of our daily living is 'detachment'. By this Eckhart means a self-freeing from all that is created, not only from the appetites which bind us to created things, but also from the *images* of created things, as we approach the point of our own self-transcendence where the world, our own created and temporal selves fall away to reveal our own bare essence, united to and unified with the Divine essence to the point of its own virtual extinction.

While Eckhart's belief in the immediacy of our union with God is one of his most attractive features as a mystical theologian, the immense weight which he lays upon the absorption of the self into God in the unitive experience was one major reason for the difficulties he experienced with the Church authorities. Christian orthodoxy requires that a distinction always be preserved between the Creator and the created (or else we fall into what is known as Pantheism), even within the context of mystical union, and there are passages in Eckhart where he seems, at best, to be oblivious to the dangers of misinterpretation on this point. The *inwardness* of his message, the all-embracing vision of divine union which forms his thought, was also a source of difficulty in that it led Eckhart to subsume the value of an external act wholly into its inner intent. Now although it is sound theology to remind us that

God judges us by our hearts, Eckhart so played down the domain of practical devotion that he laid himself open, again, to misinterpretation. Meister Eckhart has, unfairly, been read as advocating a disjunction between spiritual and moral life so that if we enjoy inner union with God, then we are no longer called to good works, and indeed, some of his contemporaries seem to have read him as saying that those who enjoy inner union with God can no longer 'sin' and are above both good and evil.

The fact that a man of Eckhart's intelligence seemed unaware of the dangers of misinterpretation is a fact which in itself requires explanation and is the result, I believe, of two factors. The first is the immensely high status as a man and scholar which Eckhart enjoyed in his own lifetime and which must have left him with a sense of his own academic invulnerability. The second factor is something akin to a sense of inebriation which we find in Eckhart. So immediate was his experience of God and so all-embracing, that Eckhart seems to have taken liberties in the exposition of his teaching, using rhetorical strategies in order to make his point and casting caution to the winds. This 'inebriation' is the *jubilatio* of the saints; it is the joy of those who know God but which, for a teaching theologian with an immense following, holds hidden perils.

JOHANNES TAULER

We may be forgiven for feeling that the Eckhartian system becomes at times a little abstract and high-flown. It is a grand, speculative system which has exercised a real fascination upon a number of fine minds across the centuries. And yet, in the daring and wonderfully expressive formulations with which Eckhart conveyed his message to the unlearned folk who flocked to hear him preach, it also attains a dramatic and poetic energy which has stirred the hearts of many. The price of such a popular packaging of subtle metaphysics however was the risk of misunderstanding, and it was indeed this which brought about Eckhart's downfall when his own boldly (and sometimes surely foolishly) formulated teachings came dangerously close to the rhetoric of unprincipled heretical movements (who advocated complete moral licence on the basis of their alleged 'union with God'). It is perhaps no wonder that the first major interpreter of Meister Eckhart sought to quieten things a bit, cautioning (interestingly) against 'inebriation', while preserving for posterity what was best in his 'noble' master's thought.

If Eckhart appeared wholly unconcerned with the possible threat of misinterpretation, then Tauler shows at every stage a keen awareness of the need to protect himself and to protect his congregations from the dangers of heretical licence based on false claims to mystical experience. Tauler is likely to have known Eckhart personally, and he certainly has a genuine understanding of the Meister's message; there are passages in his work which have an authentic Eckhartian feel. And yet there are differences. While recognizing the value of a penetrating and speculative form of mystical teaching, Tauler appears to feel that this way ('without guidance on uncharted paths'[5]) has its dangers and is for the few. Ordinary folk are better advised to go the way of the many. Tauler retains much of Eckhart's teaching, particularly his terminology, but frequently invests it with a different value and weight. The Eckhartian system, as we have seen, is a profoundly *intellective* one for which the human intellect and human cognition are pivotal. This is what lends it what has been called a sense of 'High Himalayan air' indeed, an almost Buddhist clarity and brilliance. All this is much reduced in Tauler as it is drawn towards the mainstream of Christian devotional life. Thus the Eckhartian 'spark of the soul' (so close to the Hindu teaching on Atman and the identity between the soul and God) assumes in Tauler the traditional meaning of man's inherent desire for God. The 'ground of the soul', although used frequently by Tauler, tends to take on the sense of interiority, losing something of the immediacy of its relationship to the Divine Ground, and Tauler's sense of 'mind' (*gemuet*) allows space for a psychological dimension and reality which is virtually lacking in Eckhart altogether.[6] Union with God, although central to Tauler, is also viewed in subtly different terms. He does not stress the identity of the creature and the Creator, for instance, as Eckhart had done, but hedges the point of union around with cautionary phrases such as 'if the soul could see itself, it would think that it was itself God'. Tauler also introduces the principle of grace as transforming mediation between God and the soul, and accords a place to the Holy Spirit within mystical union.

Tauler's investment of Eckhart's system with a more traditional spirituality is evident also in his handling of the 'nothingness' of creatures and of 'detachment'. The former tends now towards a sense of intrinsic moral worthlessness, guilt and sin which imposes itself upon us through the immediacy of God's presence to us, and the latter takes on a more emphatic colour as moral self-abnegation and self-denial. Suffering also comes into focus as an inevitable part of our journey and as something which can bind us into the suffering person of Christ. The sacraments likewise, particularly the Mass, assume a central position in our movement towards God. Although there is a grain of truth in the frequently repeated view that Eckhart is a 'master of thinking' (*Lehrmeister*) while Tauler is a 'master of living' (*Lebmeister*), there is a danger of over-simplification here. Tauler must not be seen as a mere appendage to Eckhart who applies his master's teaching to life; rather the relationship which obtains between them is far more complex. But we will not go far wrong if we say that Eckhart, in his terminology and in his vision of God as immediate personal encounter, is Tauler's inspiration, although Tauler's own path led him back into the trusted ways of traditional Christian devotion.

THE GERMAN THEOLOGY AND THE BOOK OF SPIRITUAL POVERTY

With these two anonymous works we arrive at a further stage in the dissemination of Rhineland (Eckhartian) mysticism. Both these texts are of a later date, and are generally thought to have been written in the early decades of the fifteenth century. They show a greater distance from the 'high mysticism' of Meister Eckhart which centres upon inner union with God, and both appear a little ill at ease with speculation.

Nevertheless these texts, which enjoyed immense popularity during the late medieval and the Reformation periods, represent a distillation of certain important Rhineland themes.

The *German Theology* (*Theologia Germanica* or *Theologia Deutsch*) lays great stress on the principle of obedience to the Divine Will, so that this becomes the basis of our spiritual life in God. Sin therefore emerges as 'self-will'. The author also knows the value of suffering, which, as for Tauler before him, becomes a way of participating in the redeeming suffering of Christ. The *German Theology* in general advocates an inward form of religion, based upon individual piety, and as such it possessed a great attraction for Protestant reformers in conflict first with the external authority of the Roman Church and, later on, in conflict with the ecclesial structures of the emergent Protestant churches.

The principal theme of the *Book of Spiritual Poverty* is that of self-stripping, a shedding both of the images of created things and of our attachments to them. With this inner poverty, which comes from a baring or denuding of the self before God, the author combines a keenly felt mysticism of suffering and of love, which draws him into the mystery of the Passion. This book also holds a special place in the Rhineland tradition for it is only here that we find a combination of inner and outer poverty in the author's explicit call to the abandonment of our property.

Neither of these two works are compositions of great originality. Even though they were greatly instrumental in the furthering of the Rhineland school in foreign lands, they represent to some extent the fading of that great tradition which found its inspiration in Meister Eckhart's singular and soaring vision. Nevertheless they provide ample material of high calibre which genuinely reflects the genius of this tradition.

JAN VAN RUUSBROEC

Ruusbroec (Ruysbroeck)[7] was not a German but a Fleming, who never left the environs of his home Brussels. Nevertheless, the social and religious situation in the Low Countries during the fourteenth century had much in common with that of the German Rhineland. The languages were cognate, even more so than today, and the great river Rhine, which flows through both areas, supported a similar culture and trade. This cultural proximity is one of the reasons why scholars have tended to assimilate Ruusbroec into the German school of the 'mysticism of Being'. Such an assimilation is supported also by the undeniable transmission of Rhineland material within the Netherlands in this period. A number of authentic sermons by Eckhart circulated anonymously, as did a version of his *Talks of Instruction* under the title *The Book of Twelve Virtues*, falsely attributed to one Godeverd van Wefele. There are strong reasons also for believing that Tauler visited Ruusbroec in his community at Groenendaal, and certainly in the year 1350 Ruusbroec sent a copy of his own *Spiritual Espousals* to the 'Friends of God' in Strasbourg, a loose association of mystically inclined folk, of which Tauler was a part. There are evident points of interdependence in the work of Tauler and Ruusbroec, which are easily explained on the basis of contacts of this kind.

The work of the unknown writer referred to as Pseudo-Hadewijch, or Hadewijch II, constitutes a further, if perplexing, link between Ruusbroec and the spiritual leaders of the German Rhineland. She was certainly known to Ruusbroec, for he quotes her in *The Twelve Beguines*, and the 'spiritual poems' of Hadewijch II show a striking similarity to the main themes of Eckhartian thought. Unfortunately the dating of these poems has proved impossible and so the problem of whether she can be said to have mediated a pure form of Eckhartian mysticism into the Netherlands remains unsolved.

Despite these points of affinity, the spiritual atmosphere of the Low Countries was subtly distinct from that of the German Rhineland. We find, for instance, a greater stress on the place of love within the mystical journey. This is the result largely of a school of spirituality which originated among the many beguine communities of women, which formed such a characteristic part of life in the Low Countries over a period of centuries. The beguines date from around the end of the

twelfth century and they differed from earlier female founda-
tions in their determination to lead an active spiritual life and
to resist regularization by the Church. They lived in celibate,
all-female communities, but their practice of remaining within
the world in order to earn their living, through a trade such
as embroidery, or even by begging, caused much concern to
the institutional church. Hadewijch of Antwerp and Beatrijs
(Beatrice) of Nazareth are the two chief literary figures in this
movement (as well as Mechthild of Magdeburg in Germany),
and their writings present a form of spirituality which places a
mysticism of love at its centre. The writings of Hadewijch and
Beatrijs, together with the Cistercian spirituality represented
by William of St Thierry's *Golden Epistle*, created in the Low
Countries a special emphasis upon the fertile role of love, in its
most practical and its most elevated forms, in our daily prog-
ression towards God. This is the tradition which fostered
Ruusbroec, despite his undeniable debt to the German Rhineland, and it is of this tradition that Ruusbroec is the sublime
culmination.

Jan van Ruusbroec stands in the tradition of a Trinitarian
love-mysticism which was conveyed to him principally by the
work of the beguines and William of St Thierry and which has
its remote origins in the thought of St Augustine. Ruusbroec
sees the human person in terms of a tripartite division: the
flesh, the mind and the spirit. Each of these three divisions
operates either according to the principle of multiplicity and
activity or of unicity and rest. Thus, for the first level of the
flesh, multiplicity and activity is expressed primarily in our
bodily faculties, which attain their unicity or rest in the centre
of our physical life, which Ruusbroec calls the 'unity of the
heart'. A second emphasis which Ruusbroec inherits from St
Augustine is the central place of grace in our life in God. It is
the workings of grace at the level of the flesh which lead us to
perform good works. This first stage of the spiritual journey
Ruusbroec calls *the active life*.

The second level is that of the mind. Here multiplicity and
activity are expressed in our higher mental faculties: our
memory, will and intelligence. These on the other hand find
their unity and rest in the 'ground' of the soul, and grace, at

this level, prompts us to a life of charity and inner devotion. Here we not only follow Christ in acts of piety and mercy, but we turn to him in our hearts and are possessed by him within. Ruusbroec calls this second stage on our path *the interior life*.

The third level, that of 'spirit', is ourselves as we exist in the Godhead. Here we encounter the source and root of our being, as we are preserved and sustained by God himself. At this highest level the principles of multiplicity and unicity, of activity and rest, are expressed in terms of the Holy Trinity, in whose life we share. Through love we are drawn into the inner life of the Trinity, becoming one with the flux of the Godhead in the Trinity, enjoying the blissful interchange of love which exists there and entering into the radiant stillness of unity as it exists beyond and within the divine persons. Ruusbroec calls this third stage of the spiritual path *the contemplative life*, and it represents the highest unitive life which is possible on earth.

Evelyn Underhill said of Ruusbroec that he was 'one of the greatest – perhaps the very greatest – of the mystics of the Church',[8] and many commentators have echoed her opinion. What makes Ruusbroec's 'system' so attractive is the combination of high speculation with an immense understanding of love. In his idea of the 'common life', Ruusbroec envisaged a circular movement which stands at the very base of his spirituality. Love draws us up and into the Holy Trinity, but love then thrusts us down again into the world so that that love may find expression and incarnation. This process of actualizing love through grace inflames us once again with love so that, through grace, we are drawn again up into the ecstatic heights of the sublime Trinity. The evidence of his contemporaries is that Ruusbroec possessed a luminous sanctity, and we can testify with them to the extraordinary power of his literary expression. If the heart experience of union with God is beyond the power of language to tell, then perhaps, of all Christian mystics at all times, it is Ruusbroec's failure which comes closest to success.

'The Ground of the Soul'

The mystics we are looking at believed that we are at the very centre of our being in some way peculiarly sensitive to God, open to him, in fact, in a way that transforms and subordinates all other aspects of our life in God. The way forward, for them, is the path of self-stripping: a denuding of the self of what is inessential so that finally we give existential priority to this hidden area deep within us in which we are drawn beyond ourselves into an immediate apprehension of God's presence. This, the idea of the 'Ground of the Soul', is certainly the most exciting aspect of the Rhineland mystics, and it is the linchpin of their spiritual teaching. It is here within the soul's 'Ground' that God himself is born, and this image, the 'Birth of God in the Soul' expresses the highest unitive state which the soul can enjoy with its Creator.

The inward thrust of the 'mysticism of essence', the belief that the place in which we come into immediate encounter with God is our own inner core, throws certain aspects of the Christian spiritual life into sharp relief. The first of these is detachment. The inner journey demands that we learn to detach ourselves from the world. Sometimes this is conceived of as a moral detachment in which we practise self-abnegation and self-abandonment, and sometimes it has the feel more of a state of consciousness in which our minds become free of all the imagery of the created world. This latter process is seen as being essential for the further advance of the soul into knowledge of the imageless and formless God. The so-called 'Negative Theology' or 'Negative Way' of the Church, according to which the utter transcendence of God is stressed, finds in the Rhineland mystics one of its richest forms of expression. In that case, the 'Ground of the Soul' is expressive of the ultimate potentiality of the soul to rise beyond knowledge of created things into a new intuited and inexpressible knowledge of the uncreated. This new way of knowing is founded not upon the exercising of a particular faculty within the soul but is itself the most inward *nature* of the soul itself. Knowledge of this kind, which is knowledge of God, is a *state of being*: it is something we *are* (though at a level far beyond our ordinary modes of 'being'), rather than something we *do*.

A second motif which gains great emphasis for these mystics of essence or being is that of poverty. The thirteenth and fourteenth centuries saw much discussion on the nature of Christian poverty; indeed, it became one of the great divisive issues of the Church in the fierce struggle between the extreme Franciscans and the Papacy. The theme which interested our mystics was, of course, that of spiritual poverty, according to which the self loses any sense of possession through its absorption into the will of God. Nevertheless, this enormously influential spiritual emphasis (which is powerfully present in the *Imitation of Christ*, for instance, and early Protestant devotional writings) must be seen as a kind of inner counterpart to the intense involvement with the issue of material poverty which exercised the Church of the day. Interestingly, the two kinds of poverty are almost never equated or seen together, but each remains oblivious of the other. The sole exception to this, as we have seen, is the *Book of Spiritual Poverty*.

The Historical Background

The reasons why Eckhart, Tauler and Ruusbroec (not to mention the author of the *Cloud of Unknowing* and the greatly influential Greek Orthodox mystic, St Gregory Palamas) lived within a few years of each other are as unfathomable as those which govern the coincidence of genius in Renaissance Italy or nineteenth century Russia. But it seems appropriate to enquire, at least briefly, what there was in the conditions of fourteenth century life which generated, or encouraged, or tolerated such a phenomenon.

First it needs to be said that the fourteenth century is a

period which has attracted from a number of scholars the language of disaster and alarm. It has been called 'calamitous' (Barbara Tuchman), 'the age of adversity' (Robert Lerner) and 'an age of unrest' (Richard Southern). It certainly suffered from more than its fair share of natural disasters as successive waves of the terrible Great Plague swept through Europe, culminating in the disastrous years of 1348 and 1349. The catastrophic destruction of the Plague led to a serious undermining of society and its institutions at all levels. It was also a time of war, with the long and painful struggle between England and France, and it was a time of great bitterness and division within the Church. For the Papacy the century had begun on a high note with Boniface VIII's bull *Unam Sanctam* (1302), which stated the Pope's claims to universal jurisdiction, even in the secular realm, in no uncertain terms. Almost immediately however the person of the Pope was seized by a band of ruffians sent by the French King, Philip IV, against whom *Unam Sanctam* had been largely directed. The church met further humiliation at the hands of the French King, whose temporal power it had unwisely challenged, when the seat of the Papacy was itself moved from Rome to the city of Avignon, where French interests could be secured. Further disasters were in store however and, in 1377, when St Catherine of Siena persuaded Clement XI to return to Rome, a tragic schism was created in the Church as his successor, Urban VI, was confronted by a rival Avignon Pope, Clement VII.

If the Papacy was seriously weakened by exile and division, by its contest with the French King and, not least, by its long struggle with Ludwig of Bavaria, who had crowned himself Emperor without papal consent, then it is also true to say that the general spiritual condition of the fourteenth century Church was notoriously bad. The example set by the Papacy and Curia was distinctly uninspiring as more and more sophisticated means of taxation were used in order to raise funds for the building of the Papal Palace at Avignon and for the waging of the Pope's Italian Wars. It is not surprising therefore that the popular heterodox movements of the day went far beyond a mere cavilling at church taxation and organization and sought to attack the heart of the Church's self-understanding. The

Bohemian Jan Hus raised a voice of challenge and protest, but the polemic launched by John Wyclif in England was a far-reaching critique of priestly orders as such and the nature of the sacraments, as well as being an attack on ecclesiastical authority.

The Brethren of the Free Spirit

Quite apart from the local tensions generated in the English Church by Wyclif and the Lollards, the fourteenth century Church was, in general, grievously exercised by the progress of powerful heretical movements no less than the thirteenth century Church had been. The latter had witnessed the rise of the Cathar and Albigensian heresies, particularly in Southern France. The death of St Francis of Assisi in 1226 had left turmoil in the Order he had founded which led to long and bitter altercations on the nature of true Christian poverty. The 'Spiritual Franciscans', as the extreme wing of the Order were called, challenged the Church's authority and became roaming bands of impassioned and disaffected men who posed a serious threat to any regular form of organized Church life. The Spiritual Franciscans however, like the Cathars before them, were a recognizable force within society with which the Church Catholic could identify and do battle. The thrust of their polemic was to set up an entirely different church organization which would oust the present one. But the same is not true of a further group, followers of the so-called heresy of the 'Free Spirit', which flourished particularly in the expanding cities of North Europe. The first description we have of this group comes from the distinguished theologian, St Albert the Great, who around the year 1270 described ninety-seven propositions which were attributable to a distinct trend which professed the 'free spirit'. It has to be said that the extent to which there was an actual movement which corresponded to this accusation, and to others, has been powerfully challenged.[9] It is difficult to judge whether there was in reality a widespread sect advocating licentiousness on the grounds of a supposed union with God, or whether this heresy existed more in the minds of the inquisitorial accusers. In particular it was the many beguine and beghard communities of North Europe who suffered accusations of heretical intent, perhaps because they tended to exist on the edge of the Church's orthodox structures or perhaps because they enjoyed a special reputation for sanctity and presented an easy target to those who envied them their standing. What makes the heresy of the Free Spirit interesting to us is that it seems to have been based upon a false claim to a special relationship with God which liberates the individual from any moral code. Adepts, it is reported, claimed that they could commit murder without incurring any guilt because their own will had been extinguished through union with the divine will, for which all was permitted. The claim to an inward state of direct union with God brought this heresy within the purview of the authentic mysticism of the Rhineland. There are without doubt superficial affinities between, for instance, some of Meister Eckhart's rhetorically formulated remarks on the 'divine spark' within the soul, or unity with the Godhead and on moral theology, and aspects of the activity and teaching of the 'Free Spirit'. As we have seen, it is tempting to view this as being one of the most likely reasons for Eckhart's downfall. The twenty-eight propositions extracted from his work which were condemned as being heretical or as 'bearing the mark of heresy' reflect in general not so much genuine theological difficulties within Eckhart's system (such as, for example, his teaching on the Trinity) but rather areas of moral teaching and teaching on the mystical state which most approximated to the heretical movement with which the Church believed itself to be engaged in a fierce struggle. Although Meister Eckhart does not himself seem alert to the possibility of such dangerous misinterpretation, it is striking that those who followed him constantly warn against it, motivated in part at least by a sound instinct for self-preservation.

A North European School of Mysticism

We might say of the mystics we have examined that their special contribution to the history of spirituality is their developed sense of the interior world of the individual, of our own inner depths and inner space. To this extent they may be said to form a characteristically North European school of mysticism, subtly distinct from that of sixteenth century Spain or seventeenth century France in its stress upon a highly developed form of interiority. The mystics of the Rhineland in fact echoed (or anticipated) in the spiritual realm the exploration of the inner man which was to become such a marked feature in the culture and the arts of North European civilization. This stress upon the individual and upon our inner depths is a trend we see in the introverted figures of the Flemish painter Rogier van der Weiden, the dramatic inner intensity of the German, Albrecht Dürer, and, of course, in the character studies of Rembrandt, which attain an incomparable psychological depth and intensity. It is anticipated also in the more profound psychology of love that we find in late medieval poets of Romance such as Walther von der Vogelweide and Gottfried von Strassburg. Although we should beware any easy identification of our mystics with the earliest tremors of the European Reformation, their positive location of the path to God within the individual person was clearly more congenial to the Lutheran focus on the inner act of faith as the foundation of our life in God than any late medieval theology of the sacraments and the external ecclesiastical order. In fact, the great Reformer was much influenced by his reading of Johannes Tauler as a young man, and himself produced two editions of the *German Theology*. Yet, even though there was much in the work of the Rhineland mystics which appealed to

Luther, including their German solidity (as distinct from the corrupting influence of alien Rome), their stress on the primacy of intent rather than action in the moral sphere, and their central focus on authentic, inner piety, they also contained elements which Luther found unwelcome. His criticism was that they were primarily God-centred rather than Christ-centred and seemed to him to be lacking in a theology of the Cross. Their concern with *Deus nudus* ('God in himself') served to distract from the engagement of the individual soul with the saving act of Christ.[10] At a later stage in the Reformation Calvin was fiercely to oppose the translation of the *German Theology*, claiming that it contained 'frivolities' and 'a hidden poison'.[11] The latter phrase may well refer to the implicit appeal to interior and individual religious feeling that we find in the *German Theology* and which was to inspire a number of Protestant groups to resist all kinds of church authority.

In part due to Protestant interest in a number of these texts and in part due to misgivings with regard to the mystical project as such and to other, more local, considerations, the Catholic Church at one time or another suppressed the works not only of Eckhart but also of Tauler and Ruusbroec, together with the *German Theology*.

Notes

1. Meister Eckhart, *Die deutschen und lateinischen Werke*, Stuttgart 1936 ff.; *Lateinische Werke* I, 132.
2. op. cit., *Deutsche Werke* I, 185.
3. op. cit., *Lateinische Werke* V, 45.
4. op. cit., *Deutsche Werke* I, 145.
5. G. Hofmann, *Johannes Tauler: Predigten*, Freiburg 1979, 104.
6. This point is well made in 'Schools of Late Medieval Mysticism' in Jill Raitt, ed., *Christian Spirituality: High Middle Ages and Reformation* (London, Routledge and Kegan Paul 1987), p. 153.
7. The name is pronounced like the English 'ruse' + 'brook'. This was the pronunciation of the original medieval form of the name (Ruysbroeck) which, however, invites a different pronunciation in modern Dutch orthography. 'Ruusbroec' therefore is a modernization of the spelling in order to preserve the original pronunciation.

8. E. Underhill, *Mystics of the Church* (1925; Cambridge, James Clarke 1975), p. 148.

9. For example, by Robert Lerner in his excellent study *The Heresy of the Free Spirit in the Later Middle Ages*, Berkeley, CA, University of California Press 1972, and by Malcolm Lambert in *Medieval Heresy*, London, Edward Arnold 1977.

10. See H. Oberman, *The Dawn of the Reformation* (Edinburgh, T. & T. Clark 1986), pp. 126–45 for an excellent review of the question of Luther and the German mystics.

11. See B. Hoffman, (ed. and tr., *The Theologia Germanica of Martin Luther*, New York, Paulist Press; London, SPCK 1980), p. 26.

PART 2

Selections

A NOTE ON THE SELECTION

Any selection of texts from writers of the highest quality will inevitably omit as much fine material as it includes. It can also happen that certain passages do not lend themselves to inclusion in an anthology of this kind for reasons of length or difficulty, or because they are dependent within the context of somebody's complete work on a specialized vocabulary. Nevertheless, the riches are there, and need only to be picked out in order to become a luminous entrance into the deep and timeless spirituality of these writers. Despite their metaphysical nature, not all that follows will be abstract; indeed, it is characteristic in general of these writers that there should be an equal emphasis on the 'nitty-gritty' of our life with God: the small, everday events which, though apparently minor, are the building blocks of a holy way of life. I have been at pains to show also this side of the 'Rhineland school', which is all too easily ignored in the excitement of a high and daring metaphysics, believing it to be the fulcrum of all else.

Meister Eckhart

Eckhart was born in the year 1260 in Hocheim in the German province of Thuringia (which is in modern day East Germany). His education began at the Dominican priory of nearby Erfurt, from where he went on to the Dominican centre for advanced studies, known as a *studium generale*, in Cologne. The major centre of learning in the late medieval world however was Paris, and sooner or later every aspiring scholar would make their way there to study at the feet of so many distinguished masters. Eckhart's first visit to Paris dates from around the year 1294 when he was a reader of Peter Lombard's *Sentences*, the standard medieval textbook of theology. From Paris he returned to his native Thuringia to act as Vicar of the province, and became Prior of his own community at Erfurt. But towards 1300 Eckhart returned to Paris, this time for studies of a more advanced kind.

If the young Eckhart proved to be an exceptionally gifted scholar, then it is clear too that he was a popular and talented administrator and organizer. The system of election to posts of responsibility within the Dominican Order was very democratic. At the beginning of the fourteenth century, the rapid expansion of the Order led to the creation of new administrative areas with their respective positions of authority. In 1304 Eckhart was put in charge of the new province of Saxony, a subdivision of the old Teutonia and, in 1307, he was also made Vicar General of the province of Bohemia, a province much in need of the attentions of an effective reformer. So successful does Meister Eckhart appear to have been that in 1310 the province of Teutonia attempted to poach him from Saxony, a move which was thwarted by the General Chapter who, in the following year, sent their distinguished theologian back to the Dominican Chair in Paris. Eckhart remained in this position for only some two years, as was the custom, and then moved to Strasburg, where he probably served as Vicar General with pastoral responsibility for the many women's convents of Southern Germany. Finally, in 1324, Meister Eckhart returned to Cologne where he took over responsibility, we may assume, for the Dominican *studium generale* there.

Eckhart's outstanding achievement as a scholar and administrator was blighted by the accusation of heresy which was made against him first of all in 1326 and which led, in 1329, to the condemnation by the Holy See of twenty-eight propositions extracted from his work. His chief accuser was Henry of Virneburg, Archbishop of Cologne, and the entire sequence of events surrounding his condemnation appear to us today to have been a distinctly unseemly exercise. We need not dwell on the details of the trial, which brought the elderly Eckhart to Avignon to make his defence, or on the condemnation itself which was drawn up without reference to the general context from which each of the *articuli* or offending propositions was taken. The underlying logic of the condemnation was the similarity between many of Eckhart's formulations on the spiritual life and the rhetoric of the Brethren of the Free Spirit (see Part One), which undoubtedly caused the Church considerable concern. The area of greatest difficulty within Eckhart's teaching from the point of view of the orthodoxy of the Church (his views on the Trinity) is not really addressed by the condemnatory Bull *In agro dominico* at all, which is simply a catalogue of statements by Eckhart which, while easily understood in an orthodox way by a sympathetic mind, lend themselves readily to a vulgar misappropriation (e.g. Art. 16: 'God does not explicitly call for external works').

Meister Eckhart possessed the skills both of a great scholar and a great popular orator. Roughly we may divide these two areas of his activity into his scholarly Latin works and his popular German works. The former are largely scriptural commentaries, which form part of the massive *Work in Three Parts*, which, however, Eckhart never completed. Their tone is generally philosophical and repetitive, in the manner of medieval exegesis, although they also contain many passages of great importance and equal beauty. The German works, on the other hand, reflect Eckhart's desire to stir his audience, to waken them to new possibilities of spiritual vision. Thus his sermons are full of challenging ideas and formulations, which have weathered the centuries well. It is largely from the German works, which are composed of numerous sermons and a number of treatises, that the present selection of texts is taken.

The following texts are broadly grouped according to themes. We begin with that of the divine spark in the human soul, which is of such great importance to Eckhart and which forms the basis whereby we attain union with God. The second group comes under the heading of 'the birth of God in the soul'. This image, which is again a central one, expresses the state of union with God which comes about when God gives birth to himself as his Son within us. This birth has the effect of making us 'detached', or free from the world with all its images of created things. This inward state of denudedness is what underlies 'poverty of spirit' also, in which our will becomes absorbed into the divine will. The remaining passages deal with diverse elements of the spiritual life, although these too, in one way or another, go back to these central, most striking, points of Eckhart's vision.

I have made these translations from *Meister Eckhart, Die Deutschen und Lateinischen Werke* (Stuttgart 1936ff), which is the standard edition of Eckhart's work and to which the sermon numbers given at the end of each passage refer. Where the required German text has not yet appeared in this edition, the reference is to Joseph Quint's *Meister Eckhart, Deutsche Predigten und Traktate* (Munich, 1936).

The divine spark I

I have occasionally said that there is a power within the soul which can alone be said to be free. Sometimes I have called it a refuge of the spirit, sometimes I have said that it is a light of the spirit, sometimes I have said that it is a spark. But now I say that it is neither this nor that, and yet still it is a something which is as high above this and that as heaven is above earth. That is why I now speak of it in a nobler manner than I have ever done before, although it mocks all my reverence and the manner of my speaking of it, and is above such things. It is free of all names and has no form; it is completely free and solitary, as God is free and solitary in himself. It is entirely unified and one, as God is unified and one, so that no one can enter it.

Sermon 2

The divine spark II

There is something which is above the created being of the soul and which is untouched by any createdness, by any nothing- ness. Even the angels do not have this, and even their pure, deep being cannot draw near to it. It is like the divine nature; in itself it is one and has nothing in common with any creature. And it is with regard to this that many teachers go wrong. It is a strange land, a wilderness, being more nameless than with name, more unknown than known. If you could do away with yourself for a moment, even for less than a moment, then you would possess all that this possesses in itself. But as long as you have regard for yourself in any way or for any thing, then you will not know what God is. As my mouth knows what colour is and my eye what taste is: that is how little you will know what God is.

Sermon 28

The divine spark III

Now see! So unified and simple is this 'fortress' in the soul, which I have in mind and of which I am speaking, so beyond particular manner, that that noble power of which I have spoken is not worthy even to glance within this fortress, not even once for a single moment, and also that other power of which I have spoken, in which God glimmers and burns with all his wealth and with all his bliss, that too does not dare glance within it. So simple and unified is this fortress, so beyond all manner and all powers is this solitary oneness, that no power or manner, no not even God, can ever find its way into it. In truth: God himself cannot enter there even for a moment, nor has he ever done so, in so far as he exists in the manner and nature of his Persons. This is easy to understand for this oneness has no manner and no nature. And therefore, if God is to enter there, then it will cost him all his divine names and the nature of his persons; he must leave them outside its walls, if he wishes to enter inside. Rather, as he is in himself One, beyond all manner and nature, he is neither Father nor Son nor Holy Spirit in this sense, and yet he is still something, which is neither this nor that.

See, he can enter this oneness, which I have called the fortress of the soul, as he is himself one and unified, and in no other way.

Sermon 2

The divine spark IV

I have spoken of a power in the soul. In its first outreach it does not grasp God in so far as he is good, nor does it grasp God in so far as he is truth. It penetrates further, to the ground of God, and then further still, until it grasps God in his unity and in his desert. It grasps God in his wilderness and in his own ground. Therefore it does not rest content with anything but seeks further for what God is in his divinity and in his own nature.

Sermon 10

The divine spark V

I have said many times already that there is a power in the soul which touches neither time nor flesh; it flows from the spirit and remains within the spirit and is of a wholly spiritual nature. Now God is in this power in a form that is just as verdant and as blooming in all joy and honour as he is in himself. We find such genuine and such great joy there that no one could ever exhaust it. For the eternal Father gives birth perpetually to his eternal Son without pause in this power in such a way that this power gives birth both to the Son of the Father and to itself as the same Son in the Father's same power. If someone were to possess a whole kingdom, or all the goods of the earth, and were to give it all up for the sake of God and were to become one of the poorest people who live anywhere on earth, and if God were then to give them as much suffering as he has ever given anyone, for all his days; if then God were to allow him to glimpse his nature as it exists in this power, his joy would be so great that he would feel that all this suffering and all this poverty had been too little.

Sermon 2

The birth of God in the soul I

The Father gives birth eternally to his Son in his own likeness. 'The Word was with God, and the Word was God': It was the same in the same nature. And I say further: he gave birth to the Word from my soul. Not only is my soul with him and he with it in his likeness, but he is in it; and the Father gives birth to his Son in the soul entirely in the same way as he gives birth to him in eternity. He must do so, whether he wishes to or not. The Father gives birth to his Son without ceasing, and I can say more: he gives birth to me as his Son and as his same Son. Further: not only does he give birth to me as his Son, but he gives birth to me as himself and himself as me and myself as him and as his nature. In the innermost source, I spring forth in the Holy Spirit; in that place there is one life, one being and one act. All God's action is one; that is why he gives birth to me as his Son, without distinction.

Sermon 6

The birth of God in the soul II

God is present, active and powerful in all things. But only in the soul is he fruitful, for all creatures are only the footprint of God, whereas the soul is by its nature modelled in God's image. This image must be ennobled and completed by this birth. No creature is responsive to this action of God and to this birth but the soul alone. Truly, whatever perfection enters the soul, whether it be divine, simple light or grace or blessedness, it can only enter the soul through this birth and in no other way. If you wait for this birth in you, then you will find all goodness and all consolation, all bliss, all being and all truth. But if you don't, then you will miss all goodness and all blessedness too. For it brings you pure being and steadfastness. And as for what you seek beyond this, the things that perish, seek them how and where you will, for they will indeed all perish. Only this gives being, all else passes away. And in this birth you will share in the divine infusion and in all God's gifts. The creatures, who do not possess the image of God, are not responsive to it, for the image of the soul belongs especially to this eternal birth, which happens specifically in the soul and is completed by the Father in the innermost part of the soul beyond all created images and faculties.

Quint, p. 425–6

The birth of God in the soul III

When this birth has really happened, then no creature can hinder you any more on your way; rather they all point you to God and to this birth. We can represent this with the image of a flash of lightning. Whatever lightning strikes, be it a tree, an animal or a man, it turns that object immediately towards it. If a man has his back towards the lightning, he turns around in that moment to face it. If a tree has a thousand leaves, they all turn instantly towards the flash. See, it is the same for those who know this birth: they are instantly turned towards it by whatever is present to them, however coarse. Indeed, what was previously an obstacle for you, now comes to your aid. Your face is completely turned towards the birth, in everything which you see or you hear, whatever it may be. You can perceive nothing but this birth in all things so that everything speaks to you of God for you have God alone in your mind's eye. It is as when we look directly into the sun so that wherever we look, we will see the image of the sun. When it is not the case that you seek God in all things and hold him before your mind's eye, then you do not yet know this birth.

Quint, p. 437

On detachment I

To be empty of all creatures is to be filled with God, and to be filled with all creatures is to be empty of God.

On Detachment

On detachment II

If therefore the heart is to be in a state of preparedness to receive the All Highest, then it must rest in nothingness, and that offers the greatest of all possibilities. Since the *detached* heart is at the highest point, then it must rest in nothingness, for that is where the greatest receptivity exists. Let me draw an analogy from nature: If I wish to write on a wax tablet, then whatever has already been written on it, however noble it might be, prevents me from writing on it, and if I wish to do so then I must first erase whatever is on it. The tablet is never better for writing on than when it is clean. It's exactly the same with God who, if he wishes to write in the highest way on my heart, must first remove everything from my heart, whatever can be called this or that, so that he is left with a *detached* heart. Then God can work within it in the highest way and according to his highest will.

On Detachment

On detachment III

In the same way, I say of those who have destroyed them-selves in themselves, in God and in all creatures that they have taken up the lowest position of all and that God must pour himself in his entirety into them, or he is not God. I swear by the eternal truth that God must pour himself to the full extent of his ability into those who have given themselves up to the ground of their being, and he must do so in such a way that he holds nothing back of his life, his being, his nature or of the fullness of his divinity. God must pour in a fructifying way all that he is into those who have given themselves up to him and who have taken up the lowest position of all.

Sermon 48

On detachment IV

As far as you depart from all things, thus far, no less and no more, does God enter into you, with all that is his . . .

Talks of Instruction

On detachment V

The whole of human perfection therefore is to become distant from creatures and free from them, to respond in the same way to all things, not to be broken by adversity nor carried away by prosperity, not to rejoice more in one thing than in another, not to be frightened or grieved by one thing more than another . . . and although this may seem to be a hard and a great thing, it is easily achieved and is necessary.

It is easy in the first place because when we have tasted of the Spirit, all things are dear to us. The immensity of the sweetness which God inspires in us extinguishes all other delights.

Secondly, because the true lover is outside God, and beyond him, as if outside being, all things are a pure nothingness.

Thirdly, because the one who loves God loves him equally in himself and for himself and has no love for anything else, then all other things will give him cause to rejoice or not to rejoice equally.

Lateinische Werke, IV 69–70

On detachment VI

Now someone who truly loves God loves him in all things and receives God, receives all things as having been willed by God, whose will is in itself the cause of delight to the one who loves God. It is as great in one thing as it is in another, in the least of things as in the greatest, in one as in all, in evil as in good, in adversity as in success, in things bitter as in things sweet . . .

Lateinische Werke, IV 66

On poverty of spirit I

God wants to be entirely our possession. This is what he wills and seeks, and that is why he is as he is. This is the cause of his greatest bliss and joy. And the more he can be our possession, the greater is his bliss and joy, for the more we are in possession of other things, the less we possess him, and the less love we have for all things, the more we receive him, with all that he offers us. Therefore when our Lord wished to speak of the beatitudes, he placed poverty of spirit at their head, and it was the first among them in order to show that all blessedness and perfection has its origin in the poverty of spirit.

Talks of Instruction

On poverty of spirit II

We must learn to remove from all God's gifts to us the sense of our own self, to possess nothing of our own and to seek nothing, neither advantage nor pleasure nor inwardness nor sweetness nor reward nor heaven itself nor our own will. God never has entered, nor ever does enter someone through their will, but only through his own will. And so wherever he finds his own will, there he gives himself and enters in with all that is his. The more we strip ourselves of ourselves, the more we become him. Therefore it is not enough that we should give up ourselves and all that we possess and all of which we are capable on one occasion alone, rather we must renew this act frequently and thus make ourselves simple and free in all things.

Talks of Instruction

On poverty of spirit III

It is written, 'You have become rich with all virtues' (1 Cor. 1.5). Truly, this can never happen until we become poor in all things. Whoever wants to receive all things, must give all things up. That is a fair trade and an equal exchange, as I once said. Therefore, because God wishes us to enjoy the possession of himself and of all things, he wishes to take from us all that is ours. Indeed, God does not desire that we should own all that we can see. For all that he has ever given us, gifts of nature as well as those of grace, was given with the intention that we should possess nothing to call our own, and never has God given anything to his mother, to any man or to any creature in any other way. And in order to instruct us and thus to provide for us, God often takes good and desirable things from us. For the possession of honour must not be ours, but his alone. We should rather possess things as if they had been lent to us, and not given: whether it be body or soul, the senses, faculties, outer goods or honour, friends, relatives, house, land or anything.

What does God intend by this, and why is he so keen that it should be so? Now he wishes to be himself our sole possession. This is his whole meaning and desire. In this lies all his yearning and delight. And the more fully and completely he can accomplish this, the greater his bliss and his joy; for the more we possess of other things, the less we possess him, and the less love we have for other things, the more we possess him with all that he brings to us. Therefore, when our Lord spoke of all the virtues, he placed poverty of spirit at their head as a sign that all blessedness and perfection have their origin in this poverty of spirit. And truly, if there were to be one ground upon which to build all goodness, then this would be it.

Talks of Instruction

On knowing God in his ground

Intellect peeps into the Godhead and searches every corner to find the Son in the heart of the Father and in his ground and thus to possess him in its own ground. Intellect forces its way into the Godhead, and is not satisfied with goodness or wisdom or truth, or even with the 'God' of creatures. In all truth, intellect is as little satisfied by 'God' as it is with a stone or a tree. It never rests but breaks into the ground from which goodness and truth emerge, and takes the divine being *in principio*, at its source, which is the point of origin of goodness and truth, before it has any name, before it proceeds forth, and the intellect takes the divine being in a far higher ground than that of goodness and wisdom. The will is satisfied with God in so far as he is good, but the intellect peels all things away, breaking in and through to the root where the Son comes forth and where the Holy Spirit burgeons into life.

Sermon 69

On our union with God

The union of God with the soul is so great that it is scarcely to be believed. And God is in himself so far above that no form of knowledge or desire can ever reach him. The desire for God reaches further than anything which can be comprehended by the intellect. It reaches further than the sky, passing beyond the angels, even though all that is on earth lives by an angelic spark. Desire is deep, immeasurably so. But nothing that the intellect can grasp and nothing that desire can desire is God. Where understanding and desire end, there is darkness and there God's radiance begins.

Sermon 42

On seeing God

If the soul is to see God, then it must see no temporal thing, for as long as the soul is conscious of time or space or of an idea, it cannot know God. If the eye is to see a colour, then it must first itself shed all colour. If the soul is to see God, then it must have nothing at all in common with nothingness. Whoever knows God, knows that all creatures are a nothingness. If we compare one creature with another, then it may appear to be something and to be beautiful; but if we compare it with God, then it is nothing.

Sermon 68

On becoming like God

In so far as we deny ourselves for God's sake and are united with God, thus far we are more God than creature. When we have fully stripped ourselves of ourselves for God's sake, and belong to no one more than we do to God and live for God alone, then truly we become through grace what God is by nature, and from his perspective God no longer perceives any distinction between us and himself.

Sermon 26

God's action

Our blessedness does not lie in our own action, but in the way that we allow God to act in us. For, just as God is nobler than creatures, so is his action nobler than ours. And it is on account of his immeasurable love that God has placed our blessedness in our capacity to allow him to act, for we can be open to his action more than we ourselves can act, and we can receive far more than we can give. Every gift demands the capacity to receive a further gift, for a greater gift, and every divine gift increases our receptivity and our desire to receive something even higher and greater. This is why some teachers say that it is in this that we see the soul's likeness to God. For the soul is as infinite in its capacity to receive as God is in his capacity to give. And God's capacity to act is as immense as our ability to allow him to act in us, which is how we are changed and transformed into him. It is for God to act as it is for us to allow him to act. Thus he is to know and to love himself in us, while we are to know and to love him with his knowledge and his love. Therefore we are much more blessed in what is his than in what is ours, and our fulfilment lies not in our action but in his.

Quint, p. 431

Seeking God for himself alone

I have upon occasion said: Whoever seeks God and seeks something else in addition to God, will not find God. But whoever truly seeks God and him alone, will find God and more than him; for they will find together with God all that he has to offer. If you seek God and seek him for your own ends or for your own pleasure, then truly, it is not God that you seek.

Sermon 26

Divine love

Whoever believes that they can escape God cannot do so, for every corner reveals him. They think that they are escaping him, but in reality they run directly to him. God gives birth to his only begotten Son within you, whether you wish him to or not, whether you are asleep or awake; he does what is his to do. I recently asked: What is to blame for the fact that we do not receive this birth? It is that our tongue is coated with dirt, that is with creatures, so we are like someone for whom all food tastes bitter. And what is to blame for the fact that the food doesn't taste nice? It is the lack of salt. Salt is divine love. If we had divine love, then God and all his works would taste sweet to us, and we would receive all things from God and would do the very things that he does. In this likeness we all become his only begotten Son.

Sermon 22

Knowing God as he is in himself

Truly, whoever believes that they receive God more in inward-ness, prayer, sweet ravishments and in the special graces of God than at the fireplace or in the stable, such a person is doing nothing other than taking God, winding a cloak about his head and thrusting him under a bench. For whoever seeks God by following one devotional path only will gain that path but miss God, who is concealed within it. But whoever in seeking God renounces all particular devotional ways, will grasp God as he is in himself. Such a person will live with the Son and will be life itself.

Sermon 5b

God is always the same

There are people who enjoy God in one way but not in another. They then only want to possess God in one way of devotion and not in another. I will say no more about this, but it is nevertheless quite wrong. Whoever wants to receive God properly must receive him equally in all things, in oppression as in prosperity, in tears as in joy. Always and everywhere he is the same.

Sermon 5a

The one gift

We must become accustomed to not seeking or striving for our own interest in anything; rather we should find and grasp God in all things. For there is no gift from God, nor has there ever been, which he gives in order that we might possess it and remain attached to it. Rather all his gifts in heaven and on earth were given solely in order that he could give the *one* gift, which is the gift of himself. With all the other gifts his intention is only to prepare us for that gift which is himself, and all the works he has done in heaven and on earth were done only that he might do the *one* work, that is to be his own delight, so that he might be the object of our delight. And so I say: We must learn to see God in all gifts and in all works, and we must not rest content with anything nor remain attached to anything at all. It cannot be right for us to linger with any particular mode of being in this life, nor has it ever been so, no matter how greatly we may have flourished by it. Above all, we should be directed towards the gifts of God, and always anew.

Talks of Instruction

On being rather than doing

You should know that we have never renounced ourselves to such an extent that we find we do not need to do so ever again. But there are few people who really understand this and who remain firm in their understanding. It is an equal exchange and a fair trade: the extent to which we leave all things is the extent, no less and no more, to which God enters into us with all that is his, in so far as we relinquish in all things what is ours. So rise up and begin to enjoy what you can. For there is true peace, and nowhere else.

People should not worry so much about what they should *do*; rather about what they should *be*. If we and our ways are good, then what we do will be radiant. If *we* are just, then *our works* will be just. We should not expect to be able to ground sanctity on what we do, but on what we are, for it is not works which sanctify us, but we who sanctify our works. However holy the things we do, they still do not make us holy in so far as they are things done but, in so far as we are holy and possess being, to that extent we make our deeds holy, whether they be eating, sleeping, waking, or whatever. Nothing comes of the deeds of those people who lack true being, whatever it is that they do. And so, take note, all our effort should be aimed at *being* good, and not so much at what we are doing or the manner of our doing, but at the ground of our works.

Talks of Instruction

On the best penance of all

Many people think that they should do great works in external things, such as fasting, walking barefoot and such like; things which we call penances. But the truest and best penance with which we make the greatest improvement, is when we turn inwardly from all things which are not God and are not divine, and turn wholly towards God in an unshakeable love so that our devotion and our desire for him become great.

Talks of Instruction

On true confidence and hope

We can tell whether our love is perfect and true by considering whether we have great hope and confidence, for there is nothing which tells us more clearly whether we have more love than trust. When someone loves another with an intense and perfect love, then that builds trust, and in God we truly find in the greatest degree those things which we dare to expect of him. If we can never love God too much, then it is also true that we can never trust him too much. And nothing we may do is as beneficial as great trust in God. For God has never failed to work great things with those who have a great trust in him. And in all these people God has made it quite clear that trust springs from love, for love not only contains trust but also true knowledge and a certainty that is free of all doubt.

Talks of Instruction

The peace of God

The extent to which we are in God is the extent to which we know peace, and without God there is no peace. Only if something is in God does it have peace. In so far as we are in God, thus far we have peace. And so we can judge whether we are in God or not, and if so to what extent we are in him, by noting whether we possess peace or not. For where we are without peace, there we cannot have peace, for the absence of peace comes from the creature and not from God. There is nothing in God of which we should be afraid, but rather all that is in him is to be loved. Nor is there anything in him which may be the cause of sadness.

Talks of Instruction

Being with God always and everywhere

I have been asked the following question. Many people with-
draw from the crowd and wish always to be alone, finding
their peace in this and in being in church. Is this the best thing
to do? I replied: No, it isn't. And this is why.

For those for whom things are right, they are right in all
places and among all people. But for those for whom things
aren't right, they aren't right anywhere or in any company.
Those for whom things are right truly have God as a companion, and whoever has God truly as a companion, is with him in
all places, both on the street and among people, as well as in
church or in the desert or in a monastic cell. No one can hinder
the person who possesses God aright. Why is this so?

It is so because such a person possesses God alone, keeping
their gaze fixed upon God, and thus all things become God for
him or her. Such people bear God in all their deeds and in all
the places they go, and it is God alone who is the author of all
their deeds. For whoever is the cause of a deed, possesses that
deed more truly than the person who performs it. If we keep
our eyes fixed on God alone, then truly he must work in us,
and nothing, neither the crowd nor any place, can hinder him
in this. And so nothing will be able to hinder us, if we desire
and seek God alone, and take pleasure in nothing else.

Talks of Instruction

The light of God in the soul

But the ways in which this light ought to enter are barred and blocked by falsity and by darkness. Now light and darkness cannot coexist any more than God and creatures can: if God is to enter, then the creature must depart. And so we become aware of the light. Whenever we turn to God, a light shines forth in us, letting us know what it is that we should do and not do, and giving us many more previously unknown instructions. 'But how do you know this?' – Now listen! Your heart is often touched in this way and turns from the world. How could that happen, if not by this light? It happens so quietly and so sweetly that everything which is not God or of him begins to oppress you. You are drawn to God, and are filled with many good intuitions which come from you know not where. This inward inclination towards God does not come from any creature or from any prompting from them, for what comes from creatures comes always from outside. But your ground is touched only by this illumination from within, and the more you strip yourself of yourself, the more light and truth and clarity you will find.

Quint, p. 426

Johannes Tauler

Tauler was born in the flourishing Rhineland town of Strasburg around the year 1300. Like Eckhart before him, he joined
the local Dominican community as a boy of some fifteen years,
where he would have received a basic training in the Arts and
in Theology. Unlike Eckhart, however, there is no evidence
that Tauler ever showed the skills to take him to the Dominican
studium generale in Cologne for a higher education. He does not
write in Latin, the language of the medieval scholar, and
indeed he shows an unmistakable suspicion of book learning
at times. But whatever the nature of his formal training,
Tauler's grasp of theological realities is deep and, probably
around the year 1325, he was ordained a Dominican priest.

One reason for the immense popularity which Tauler enjoyed during his own lifetime may have been the fact that he
travelled around a good deal. In 1339 his own community was
forced to leave Strasburg for Basle as a result of a papal
interdict on that city, which opted for loyalty to the Emperor
Ludwig in his struggle with Pope John XXII. Tauler also visited
Cologne in 1339 and 1346, and it is more than likely that he
travelled to Groenendaal, near Brussels, in order to visit the
Flemish mystic of renown, Jan van Ruusbroec. Another
journey, this time to Paris, is disputed.

Tauler fell ill in 1360 and, according to one tradition, was
cared for by his sister, a Dominican nun. He died on 16 June,
1361. His tombstone can be seen in the Lutheran church
in Strasburg, which was built on the site of the original
Dominican church which was destroyed by fire in 1870.

Tauler's eighty-four sermons have come down to us in the
form of *reportationes*, which are transcriptions made by those
who heard him speak, although it is very likely, on account of
their form and clarity, that the preacher himself scrutinized the
end product. The first printed edition of these sermons was in
Leipzig in 1498 but the later edition with which Tauler's work
reached its greatest audience was the Latin translation by
Laurentius Surius printed in Cologne in 1548. This was the
edition which took Tauler's thought as far afield as Spain,
where it exercised a not inconsiderable influence (although

there is no evidence that it was known to St John of the Cross). This edition also contained a number of sermons actually by Meister Eckhart which were thus circulated under Tauler's name.

It was the edition printed in Augsburg in 1508 which Martin Luther read and by which he was greatly impressed. He referred to 'such sterling theology, equal to that of the ancients' (letter to Spalatin, 14 December 1516, *Wiemar Ausgabe* I, 30, 58). He admired Tauler's apparent suspicion of works, his advocacy of complete submission to God's will and his remarks on the sufferings which befall the devout soul with which Luther identified his own sense of alienation from God. But Luther's mistrust of Tauler's essentially mystical teaching is clear from his substitution in the Augsburg text of the word 'Faith' for the latter's 'Spark of the soul' (*Wiemar Ausgabe* IX, 99, 36).

The selection which follows begins with texts on the 'ground of the soul'. The 'ground', for Tauler, is the essence of our soul and it is the place where we come into direct contact with the Divinity. Tauler differs from Eckhart in that he allows more space to the human soul, but he is emphatic that we are driven at this deep level by an insatiable hunger for God and predisposition to receive him. The following texts stress that we must give up selfishness and our own self-will if we are to be united with God, and Tauler emphasizes the place of Christ in that process. As for Eckhart, the attitude we must learn is essentially one of passivity, and of allowing God to work in us. Perhaps more than any other mystic of his age, Tauler is aware that God's work in us can be a form of suffering (an important anticipation of the 'Dark Night of the Soul' of St John of the Cross.) Indeed, in general Tauler stresses the immense spiritual value for us of our everyday tribulations, and how these serve to distinguish the true witness from the false. Tauler shows a great understanding, in fact, of the periods of weakness and failure which affect us all. The selection concludes with some marvellous extended images, in which Tauler speaks of profound matters of the spirit in imagery drawn from everyday life in the Rhineland.

No standard critical edition of Tauler exists. I have based the present translations on Corin's *Sermons de J. Tauler et autres écrits mystiques* (Paris 1924–9) and Vetter's *Die Predigten Taulers* (Berlin 1910). The modern German edition by G. Hoffman, *Johannes Tauler: Predigten* (Freiburg 1979), is also an important source. The number of the sermon given after each passage refers to the numbering followed by Hoffman and Corin.

The ground of the soul I

The soul bears within a spark, a ground, whose thirst almighty God cannot satisfy, unless it be by giving himself. If he were to give the soul the spirit of the forms of all things that he has created in heaven and earth, then this would not be enough and could not satisfy this thirst, which the soul possesses by its nature. Those perverse people then destroy this ground within themselves, they stifle this thirst and open their mouths wide as if they believed the wind could satisfy them. And thus they have no taste for the things of God.

Sermon 36

The ground of the soul II

St Augustine says of this ground that the soul of man possesses a hidden abyss which has nothing whatever to do with time and this world and which is raised far above the part of us which gives life and movement to our body. The delight of which we have spoken descends into that noble, blissful abyss, into that hidden domain, which is its resting place for all eternity. There we become so still, so true to ourselves, so clear in judgement, so detached and so inward. There we are renewed in purity and renunciation, set free from all things, for God himself enters that heavenly domain, where he acts, dwells and rules. This condition cannot be compared with any other, for in this we attain to a truly divine life. Our spirit fuses wholly with God, burns in all things and is drawn into the fire of love which is God himself according to his essence and his nature.

Sermon 24

The ground of the soul III

In the abyss the spirit of man loses itself so utterly that it is no longer conscious of itself: neither of its words or its ways, its impressions or feelings, its knowledge or love, for everything is pure undivided God, an inexpressible abyss, one essence, one spirit. God gives through grace to the human spirit that which he is by his nature, and unites with the human spirit his own being, without name, manner or form. And God will cause all the works of this soul, knowing, loving, praising and enjoying them, as the soul allows him to do so in a God-suffering manner. We can speak as little of this and of how it happens as we can speak of and understand the divine being itself, for this is an order of knowledge too high for the created intellect, of man or angel, even when illumined by God's grace.

Sermon 26

The ground of the soul and Christ

We should strive further and reach higher the deeper we sink into the unknown and unnamed abyss. Here we lose ourselves completely, are stripped of all images, all manners of devotion, all forms, and go beyond all our powers. And so finally there is nothing left but the ground, which exists essentially within itself, one being, one life, one transcendence. We can say of this state that we are freed from all knowledge, all affection, all action, yes even from the spirit. This is not an oddity of nature but happens on account of the transformation which the spirit of God works in the created spirit in a free act of goodness, corresponding to the unfathomable abandonment of the created spirit and its deepest detachment from all things. Of such people we can say that God knows himself in them, loves himself, delights in himself in them, for he is one life, one being, one energy. Should someone ever wish to tread this path with a false freedom and in a false light, then that would be the most perilous way of conducting themselves.

The way which takes us to this point must lead through the sacred life and suffering of our Lord Jesus Christ, for he is the way, and this is the way that we must go. He is the truth which must illumine this way, and he is the life which we must attain. He is the doorway, and whoever wishes to enter through another door is a thief. We should enter through this beloved door by disciplining our nature, and by practising the virtues, in humility, gentleness and patience. Know in truth: those who do not choose this path shall lose their way. God goes before those people who do not take this path, he walks even in their midst; yet still they are blind.

Sermon 64

Johannes Tauler | 69

The birth of God in the soul

Truly, there must be a movement within if that birth of God in the soul is to happen. There must be a decisive act of turning within, a retrieval, an inner unification of all our powers, the lowest and the highest, a gathering of the self in the face of all distractions, for those things which are unified are stronger than those which are not. It is just as when a bowman, who wants to hit a target exactly, closes one eye in order that the other can see more clearly. Whoever wants to observe something closely, should apply all their senses to it, unifying them within the soul, which is their source. Just as all the branches of a tree emerge from its trunk, in the same way all the powers of the soul, those of the senses, of feeling, of the will are unified at the highest point, in the ground of the soul. And this is recollection.

If we are to escape from ourselves, if we are to be raised above and beyond ourselves, then we must renounce all selfish intents, desires and actions. Our will should be directed towards God alone, and there should exist within us nothing of our own selves, our own becoming and our own gain. We should belong only to him, yielding space to him who is the highest of all for us and the nearest, so that his work may flourish and his birth in us be completed, without us hindering him in any way.

Sermon 1

Learning silence

If you want to be taken up into God's inmost nature, to be transformed into him, then you must free yourself of yourself, of your nature, your inclinations, your actions, your self-opinion, in short of all the ways in which you have had possession of yourself. For with these it cannot work. Two beings, two entities cannot occupy the same space. If warmth is to enter, then the cold must leave. Is God to find a way in? Then created things and all that which is in your possession must make a space for him. If God is really to be active in you, then you must enter a state of true passivity. All your faculties must be stripped of their action and their self-assertion and you must maintain yourself in a pure denial of yourself, deprived of all force, dwelling in a pure and absolute nothing-ness. The more we become nothing, the truer and more essential is our union with God. And if it ever became as pure and as essential as is the case with the soul of our Lord Jesus Christ – which of course is not possible – then our union with God would be as great as is Christ's union with him. We become God in so far as we lose ourselves. If God is truly to speak to you, then all the energies of your soul must be silent. It is not a question of learning to *do*, but of learning *not to do*.

Sermon 31

On accepting God's will

How few people we find in the world who do not have regard only for themselves, who do not lean on the supports of their own being, who hope for nothing, seek nothing but the perfection of God's will in them. This they do in no other way than that of which our Lord spoke when he said: 'When you have done all that is in your power, then say: "We are useless servants".' A useless servant does nothing of value, and yet we constantly want to be assured that we have done something worthwhile. That is what we build on secretly, and that is our wish. But no, what we should build on in truth is our own complete nothingness, casting ourselves into the abyss of the divine will, accepting whatever it is that he wishes to do with us. Do as St Peter did when he said: 'Lord, leave me, for I am a sinner.' We should sink to our knees at our own small-ness, our impotence, our ignorance, giving ourselves over into the great nobility of God's will. We should keep all else at bay, remaining poor and wretched in his will. When people of this kind turn within to the ground of their soul for the length only of a Mass, then they have achieved all their works and, from that point onwards, all that they do will possess great peace, and their whole life will be still and virtuous, gentle and serene and full of goodness.

Sermon 42

Detachment

Now what does 'true detachment' mean . . . ? It means that we should turn and detach ourselves from all that is not God alone, that we should examine with the light of reason all our works, words and thoughts to see whether there is not something in the ground of our soul which is other than God and which does not hunger for God in all things, in activity as in passivity. And should we find anything which is directed at something other than God, then we should cut it off and cast it out.

Sermon 23

Two things

If you want to become perfect and to achieve the best that you are capable of, then keep these two points in mind. The first is that you should free your inner heart of all created things, including yourself, and that you should control your inner and your outer self so that you do not obstruct the work of the Holy Spirit in you. The second is that you should accept difficulties, whatever their cause, be they inner or outer, and whatever their nature, as coming from God and in no other way, for God thereby wishes to make you for himself and to enable you to receive his great gifts, which are supernatural and wonderful and to which you could never attain except by suffering patiently the effects of the enemy and of hostile men.

Sermon 25

Humility

And so above all we must enter our own nothingness. If we were to reach the very pinnacle of all perfection, then it would be even more important that we should sink into the deepest ground, to the very roots of humility. For as the height of a tree depends on the depths of its roots, in the same way the heights we attain in this life are only as great as our humility is deep.

Sermon 48

Humility through suffering

The sort of person God wants us to be is humble and gentle, poor in spirit and pure, detached from all things and of enduring serenity. This does not mean that we should sit down and hide our heads. Not at all! But we should let God seek us out, weigh upon us and destroy us so that we learn humility in all life's situations wherever or through whomever it comes. Whoever seeks something that they have lost does not look for it only in one place but in many places, here and there, until it is found. See, so you too must seek God in many different ways. Allow him to find you in all the turns of fate, in all the events that happen to you, whatever or whoever is their cause. Whatever derision, whatever humiliation befalls you, accept it as coming from God, for it is in this way that he seeks you.

Sermon 36

The true witness I

There are many who wish to be God's witnesses in time of peace, when all things are going as they would wish them to, and these people would gladly be holy, as long as their spiritual exercises and efforts do not turn sour on them. But when great tribulations come upon them, when darkness comes and they cannot feel or sense the presence of God, when they feel abandoned both within themselves and in the circumstances of their lives, then they do an about-turn and show that they are not God's true witnesses. All of us seek peace and seek it everywhere, in what we do and what we are. If only we could start again and begin to seek peace in the absence of peace – for that alone is where true and lasting peace is born, and whatever else you seek is illusion, even when it is peace. We should begin to seek joy in grief, serenity in impermanence and consolation in bitterness. This is the way to be God's true witness. He promised his disciples peace before his death and after his resurrection, and yet they never found external peace, but discovered peace where there was none and joy where there was grief. In death they found life and joyful victory, even as they were brought before the judge, and were condemned. These were the true witnesses of God.

Sermon 21

The true witness II

Those, however, who are God's true witnesses rely upon God in the good and the bad and they rely stoutly upon his will, whether he gives to them or takes from them. They do not hold to their own intentions. And so if they think that they can perform great things and begin to count upon that, then God will frequently undermine whatever it is that they do because he means well with them, and thus things frequently happen which were not desired. If we wish to stay awake in vigil, then we must sleep against our will, if we wish to fast, we must eat, if we wish to remain in silence and in peace, then things happen quite differently. Thus, every form of fixity is broken, and we are turned back upon our own nothingness, and are dependent upon God, acknowledging him in simple, humble faith and renouncing all fixity.

Sermon 21

Suffering and the true friends of God

We can tell whether people have the true love of God when great sufferings befall them. The friends of God take them to God and suffer them for his sake. They accept them as coming from him so that they suffer them with him or in him. Or they so lose themselves within him, because God unites himself so inwardly with them, that suffering in God ceases for them to be suffering at all, but becomes a joy and a delight. But if suffering befalls the false friends of God with their pharisaic ways, then they do not know which way to turn but run all about the place, seeking help, counsel and consolation. And when they do not find these, then they go to pieces and fall into despair.

Sermon 10

The value of temptations

In temptation we are made aware of the ground of our own soul. What value temptations must have! If we perceive this truth, then they will become as necessary for us as the virtues are. We need temptations as we need grace. In temptation virtue is gained, and in temptation it is perfected. This has to be so if virtue is to become fully realized. We are subject to temptation in all the circumstances of our inner and outer lives. A scholar has written: 'We need temptation just as meat needs salt in order to remain free from corruption.' God can take possession of us through temptation as he can through the virtues or the holy sacraments. When temptation exposes the stain and the roots of sin, then these are torn out, humility is born by the fear of God, and we are urged to flee to God, to seek his help and to hand our battle against sin over to him.

Sermon 75

The absence of God

All people desire this true celebration of eternal life by nature, for all people desire by nature their own happiness. But this desire is not enough on its own: we must strive for God and seek him. Many would greatly like this foretaste of the high feast to come and they complain that it is withheld from them. They feel no sublime joy in the ground of their soul when they pray and, when they cannot feel the presence of God, they become vexed and pray less often or less lovingly, saying that they do so because they cannot feel God's presence. This is not what we should do. We should not do anything less diligently, for God is truly present with us. Even if we do not know it, he comes quietly to the celebration. And where God is, there is the high feast, and he cannot refrain or abstain from coming. He simply has to be there when someone strives towards him and seeks him alone. Though at times secretly, yet he is always there.

Sermon 12

The inner life

But each time that you are granted the solemn moment of recollection, leave your outer forms of devotion to one side, if they become a hindrance to you, for inner prayer is precious divine life. Concentrate upon what leads you most to love, for instance the life, the suffering, the divine wounds of Christ, God's essence, the Blessed Trinity, the power, the wisdom, the goodness of God, the good things which he has done for you. Whatever stirs you most, go with that, full of gratitude, into the ground of your soul, and wait for God there. Doing this, with love, enables us to receive God much more effectively than any outer spiritual exercise. The more inward something is, the better it is, for the external things derive all their value from what is within. It is as if you had a good wine which was strong enough to change a whole tun of water into best wine. It is the same with the life within, a single drop of which can lend our life of external devotion a higher value.

Sermon 39

Following Christ

Beloved St Matthew is a fine model for us all. Previously, however, he had been a great sinner, as Scripture says, before becoming one of the greatest friends of God of all, for our Lord spoke to him inwardly, in the ground of his soul so that he left everything and followed him. This is the all-important thing: that we should follow God in truth. This means letting go of everything which is not God, whatever it may be, letting go of what is in the ground of our soul and has possession of us, whatever that may be, living or dead, we ourselves, or some form of self-possession. For God loves hearts and is not concerned with what can be seen from the outside but with an inner, living assent to him, which possesses a ready inclination towards all that is godly and virtuous, wherever it may be. This is a truer and more righteous attitude than if I were to pray as much as everyone else in the world put together of if I were to sing so loudly that my voice carried all the way to heaven and it is better than everything I could possibly achieve in terms of fasting and vigils and other forms of pious exercise.

Sermon 64

The Holy Spirit

This precious Holy Spirit entered the disciples and all those who were open to him, bringing such wealth, such abundance and superfluity, and overflowed them inwardly. It was as if we were to allow the Rhine its way, removing from its path all hindrances. As if it were to break its banks with its mass of flooding waters, roaring and threatening to submerge all things, filling all the valleys and inclines. So too did the Holy Spirit come upon the disciples and all those who were open to him. And so he still does today unceasingly; he fills and floods the grounds of our souls, our hearts and minds, whatever he finds. These he fills with great wealth, graces, love and indescribable gifts. And thus he fills the valleys and the depths which are opened up to him.

Sermon 25

The highest love

The gold with which we compare this, the highest form of love, is so brilliant and so radiant that we can hardly look at it. Its brightness is too strong for the eyes. It is the same for our spirit and this mighty love in which the Lord himself is present. It shines so brightly and essentially in the ground of the soul that the spirit in its human weakness cannot bear to gaze upon it, but must necessarily dissolve and return to its former powerlessness. Then the spirit has no more supports but sinks and falls away into the divine abyss and so loses itself in it that it has no more knowledge of itself, for the image of God, which corresponds to this love, overwhelms it. And then it does exactly what Elijah did at the mouth of the cave, that is to say, in his human weakness at the door of God's presence. He drew his cloak over his eyes, which means that the spirit loses its own form of knowledge and its own reality. Now God must work all things in us; it is he who knows and loves within us, for in this mighty love the human spirit falls away from itself, losing itself in the beloved like a drop of water in a deep ocean. It has become more united to God than the air is with the light of the sun. What this is must be experienced, for it cannot be spoken of.

Sermon 52

The fruit of repentance

The horse drops dung in the stable. Although the dung is unclean and evil smelling, the same horse laboriously pulls the same dung to the fields where fine wheat and good sweet wine grow from it, which would never grow so well if the dung were not there. Now, your own faults, of which you cannot rid yourself or overcome are your dung. These you should carry with much effort and labour to the field of God's will in true detachment from yourself. Scatter your dung on this noble field and, without any doubt, there shall spring up noble and delightful fruit.

Sermon 6

The noble fruit

What noble and precious fruit God grows from those who cultivate their vine in such a way that the divine sun can work upon it and penetrate it! Then the sun shines and works upon the grape and brings it to glorious fruit . . . Then the sun shines more brightly still and casts its heat upon this fruit and makes it more and more transparent, the sweetness in it grows and the skin of the fruit becomes ever thinner so that the inside is constantly exposed to God's view. However often we turn towards it, we always find that it is illumined by the divine sun from within, more clearly than any sun ever shone in the sky, and thus all our ways are transformed into God so that we neither perceive nor delight in any thing nor know any thing more truly than God, though in a manner which transcends the powers of reason and rational knowledge. And then the leaves are stripped away so that the sun can shine upon the fruit fully. In the same way all obstacles will fall away from such a person and they will receive everything without hindrance. Now prayer falls away, the image of the saints, all forms and practices of devotion. And yet we should not let these go before they fall away of their own accord. Thereupon the fruit becomes so inexpressibly sweet that no intelligence can comprehend it and it comes to the point that the spirit of this person enters the deeps where there is no more distinction. Thus we become one with the sweetness of the Godhead, our being so permeated by the divine being that we lose ourselves as a drop of water is lost in a vat of wine. Our spirit is so immersed in God in divine unity that we lose all sense of distinction, we lose all that brought us to this point, our name, humility and love, our very selves. Then there reigns a pure, still, hidden unity without any distinction. Here mind and humility become simplicity, an essential, still hiddenness that defies comprehension. To dwell there for a single hour, even for a moment, is a thousand times more profitable and more valuable to God than forty years of clinging to your own desires. That this may be so for us too, so help us God.

Sermon 7

Jan van Ruusbroec

Ruusbroec was born in 1293 in or around the city of Brussels in modern-day Belgium. His studies began in the chapter school of St Gudule, the principal church in Brussels (and which is now the cathedral church dedicated to St Michael), where he was ordained priest in 1317. In 1343, however, the low standards prevailing in church life in the city drove him and two friends away from Brussels to Groenendaal ('Green Dale') in the forest of Soignes to the south-east of the city. Here they founded a small community where they felt they could pursue a spiritual life unhindered by the extensive compromise with the world which was so often characteristic of the Church in the fourteenth century. Their intention, it seems, was successful, and in course of time they were joined by a number of others to aid them in their project. In 1349 they 'regularized' their new way of life by adopting the Augustinian Rule.

Under the influence of Ruusbroec, and others, Groenendaal became a celebrated centre of pilgrimage. As we have seen, Tauler is likely to have visited the forest monks, and it is certain that Geert Groote (Gerard Grote) did so. Groote is remembered today as the founder of the Brethren of the Common Life (a congregation who were to influence both Erasmus and Luther) and as a key figure in the spread of the Modern Devotion, which as a popular movement of spiritual reform found its highest expression in Thomas a Kempis's justly celebrated *Imitation of Christ*.

At Groenendaal Ruusbroec continued the work of spiritual writing which he had begun in Brussels where, in fact, he had written his most famous book, *The Spiritual Espousals*. Ruusbroec wrote altogether eleven treatises on the spiritual life, many of which took the form of scriptural exegesis. But, whatever the manner of his writing, he consistently dealt with the same theme of absorption into the inner life of the Trinity through love. The process of translating the works of Ruusbroec from Flemish into Latin, thus making them available for everyone, began early on. It was the Cologne Carthusian Laurentius Surius, however, who in the sixteenth century gave the Latin translation of Ruusbroec its final form, as he did also for Tauler, and it was in the Surius translation that Ruusbroec became known all over Europe. As early as the fourteenth century, however, extracts from two of his works were circulating in England in English translation, primarily within the Carthusian Order. One of these, *The Chastizing of God's Children*, may well have exercised an influence on the English spiritual tradition at an important stage in its development.

The following selection of texts from Ruusbroec's works reflect his tripartite division of human kind, and his belief that the spiritual path knows three distinct stages. The first stage corresponds to the 'outer man' and is concerned with acts of virtue and good works. This stage is known as the 'Active Life'. The second stage, the 'Interior Life', is more inward and devotional, and is concerned with movements of love towards God and the inner life of grace. The final stage is that of the 'Contemplative Life' (or 'God-seeing Life') in which we are drawn up, through love, into the inner flux and rhythms of the Trinity itself. This is the highest experience which we can know on earth, and it corresponds to that part of us which itself receives the imprint of the Divinity.

My translations of Ruusbroec's work are taken in the main from the edition by Poukens *et al.* called *Werken* (Tielt, 1944–8). Translations from *The Little Book of Enlightenment* and *The Seven Enclosures* are taken from the, as yet incomplete, new edition by Alaerts *et al.*, *Jan van Ruusbroec: Opera Omnia* (Leiden/Tielt, 1981ff).

The active life: purity of intention

Now understand how we can meet God in each of our works, increasing in our likeness to him and more nobly possessing our blissful unity with him. Every good work, however small it may be, which is performed in God with love and a righteous, pure intention, earns for us a greater likeness to God and eternal life in him. A pure intention unites the scattered powers of the soul in the unity of the spirit and orientates the spirit towards God. A pure intention is the end and beginning and adornment of all virtue. A pure intention offers praise and honour and all virtue to God. It passes through itself, the heavens and all things and finds God in the purity of its own ground. That intention is pure which holds only to God and sees all things in relation to God.

The Spiritual Espousals 209

The active life: encountering God through virtue

In this way we should live in the unity of our spirits in grace and in likeness to God, encountering God constantly through the intermediary of virtue and offering our life and all our works in purity of intention to him so that we shall at all times and in all our works become more like him. And so, on the foundation of our pure intention, we shall transcend ourselves and meet God without intermediary and rest with him in the ground of simplicity. There we shall possess the inheritance which has been preserved for us from all eternity.

The Spiritual Espousals 210

The active life: giving up self-will

From this obedience there comes the renunciation of our own will and our own opinions. Only those who are obedient can deny their own will in all things for the will of another, for anyone can do outer works and yet hold to their own will . . . By renouncing our own will in deciding what is to be done, what not done and what is to be endured, the substance and occasion of pride is banished and humility is perfected in the highest degree. And God becomes master of a person's whole will, which becomes so united with God's will that he or she can neither will nor desire anything else.

The Spiritual Espousals 125

The active life: the acceptance of suffering

If people are to be healed of this distress they must feel and think that they are not their own possession but that they belong to God. And therefore they must abandon their own self-will to the free will of God, allowing God to act in time and in eternity. If they can do this without heaviness of heart and with a free spirit, then at that very moment they will be healed and bring heaven to hell and hell to heaven. For however much the scale of love goes up and down, they always remain perfectly balanced. For they who suffer without resentment remain free and balanced in their spirit, and they experience the union with God without intermediary.

The Little Book of Enlightenment 126

The active life: God within

All grace and all gifts flow forth from this unity in which the spirit is unified without intermediary with God . . . This grace descends on us in the unity of our higher powers and our spirit from which these flow out in active virtue by means of grace and to which they return again in the bond of love . . . Now the grace of God, which flows forth from God, is an interior impulse or urging of the Holy Spirit which drives our spirit from within and urges it outwards towards all the virtues. This grace flows from within us and not from outside us, for God is more interior to us than we are to ourselves and his interior urging and working within us, whether natural or supernatural, is closer and more intimate to us than our own activity. For this reason God works from within us outwards, whereas all creatures act upon us from without.

The Spiritual Espousals 147

The interior life: encountering God without intermediary

Sometimes those who live the interior life turn in within themselves in a simple manner following their inclination to delight, and there, beyond all activities and virtues, they look with a simple and inward gaze upon blissful love. Here they meet God without intermediary. And there shines upon them from the depths of God's unity an undifferentiated light, which shows them darkness, bareness and nothingness. Such people are enveloped in the darkness and fall into modelessness as if they were quite lost. In the bareness they lose the perception and distinction of all things and are transformed and permeated by a simple radiance. In the nothingness all their works fail them, for they are overwhelmed by the activity of the love of God that is deep without end. And in the inclination towards delight of their spirit, they overcome God and become one spirit with him. And in this union in the spirit of God they savour an ecstatic delight, and possess the divine essence.

The Spiritual Espousals 223

The interior life: the fury of love

And the soul lays open all her faculties in order to give God all that she is and to receive from him all that he is. But this is impossible for her. The more she gives and receives, the greater her desire to give and to receive. And she can neither give herself to God entirely nor receive God entirely. For all that she receives, compared with what she still lacks, is little and it seems to her to be nothing. Therefore she becomes tempestuous and falls into restlessness and a deep fury of love, for she can neither do without him nor acquire him, neither sound his depths nor scale his heights, neither embrace him nor abandon him. But where the human way is found wanting and can go no higher, there begins the way of God. That is, when we hold to God with intention, with love and with unsatisfied desire and cannot become one with him, then the Spirit of Our Lord comes like a mighty fire that burns, consumes and devours all that is in us so that we are no longer aware of ourselves and our devotions but we experience ourselves as if we were one spirit and one love with God.

The Seven Enclosures 182

The interior life: hunger and thirst for love

Sometimes those living the interior life turn actively and with desire towards God so that they can give God all glory and honour, offering God themselves and all their works, and thus they are consumed in God's love . . . they have an inward perception and sensation in the ground of their being, where all virtues have their beginning and their end and where they offer God all virtues with desire, and where love dwells. Here the hunger and thirst of love become so great that they surrender themselves at every moment and cannot work, but rather transcend their activity and are destroyed in love. They hunger and thirst for the taste of God and at each sight of him they are grasped by him and touched by him anew in love. So living they die, and dying they return to life. Thus the yearning hunger and thirst of love are constantly renewed in them.

The Spiritual Espousals 225

The interior life: love's mastery

You well know that I have already said how all the saints and all good people are united with God with intermediary. Now I want to go on to tell you how they are all united with God without intermediary. But there are few in this life who are able and enlightened enough to feel and understand this. And for this reason, whoever wishes to feel and experience within themselves these three forms of union with God of which I speak, must live for God with their whole selves so that they can respond to the stirrings and grace of God, and submit to him in all virtues and interior exercises. They must become exalted through love and die in God to themselves and to all their works so that they yield with all their faculties and suffer the transformation of the unfathomable truth which is God himself. Thus they must go out, living, to the practice of virtue and, dying, enter into God . . . Because they thus hold and exercise themselves in the presence of God, love will master them in every way.

The Little Book of Enlightenment 122

The interior life: the storm of love

In the summer it is common to see two strong opposing winds clash and storm together in the air, thus creating thunder and lightning, hail and rain, sometimes even tempests and plagues, here below. We can see the same thing in the storm and fury of love when the human spirit is raised up to union with the spirit of Our Lord and each spirit touches the other with love and each makes invitation to the other and offers it all that it is and all that it can do. Then reason is enlightened and becomes clear and desires at all cost to know what love is, and what that touch may be that moves and wells up in the spirit. And desire wants to discover and savour all that the enlightened reason can know, which gives rise to a storm of love in the soul and great restlessness. But this the loving spirit well knows: the more it gains, the more it lacks. And the storm and fury of love which spring forth, burning and welling up within it, cannot be appeased, but from each mutual renewing touch come yet more storms of love. And these storms are just like thunderclaps from which there springs the fire of love, like sparks from gleaming metal and fiery lightning from heaven.

The Seven Enclosures 176

The interior life: the touch of God

Thus similarly the grace of God floods into the higher powers like streams, driving and inflaming a person to the practice of all virtues. And it dwells in the unity of our spirit like a spring, welling up in this same unity from which is arises, just like a living vein welling up out of the living ground of God's richness where neither faith nor grace can ever fail. This is the touch that I mean.

The creature undergoes this touch passively for here is the union of the higher powers in the unity of the spirit, above the multiplicity of all virtues. And no one is active here but God alone, in his sovereign divinity, who is the cause of all our virtue and blessedness. In the unity of the spirit, where this vein wells up, we are above all works and above reason, but not without reason, for the enlightened reason, and especially the power of love, feel this touch though reason cannot grasp or understand the mode or manner of this touch, or how or what it is. This is because the touch is a divine work, the source and eruption of all graces and all gifts, and it is the last intermediary between God and creature.

The Spiritual Espousals 196

The interior life: love's penetration

And those who, through the practice of virtue and interior exercises, have fathomed the depths of their being to its source, which is the door to eternal life, are able to feel the touch. There the radiance of God is so great that reason and all the powers of understanding fail, having to suffer and yield to the incomprehensible radiance of God. But the spirit who feels this touch in its ground finds that, although its reason and understanding fail before the divine radiance and must remain outside the door, the power of love wills to go further. Like the intellect, it has been called and invited but, being blind, desires only to enjoy; and enjoying is more a matter of savouring and feeling than understanding. This is why love enters while understanding remains outside.

The Spiritual Espousals 198

The contemplative life: the abyss of love

You can thus see that the attractive power of the unity of God is nothing other than love without end which, through love, draws the Father and the Son and all that lives in them into an eternal delight. And we desire to burn and be consumed in this love for all eternity, for it is here that the blessedness of all spirits lies. Therefore we should found our whole life on a fathomless abyss so that we eternally sink into love and immerse ourselves in its fathomless depths. And in the same love we will rise up and rise above ourselves to an incomprehensible height. In this modeless love we will wander, and it shall bring us into the immeasurable breadth of God's love. There we shall flow forth and flow out of ourselves into the uncomprehended abundance of God's riches and goodness. There we will melt and be dissolved, eternally taken up into the maelstrom of God's glory.

The Sparkling Stone 8

The contemplative life: entering the Trinity

Therefore God has given us a life above ourselves, and that is a divine life. It is nothing other than a contemplating and a gazing and a holding to God in bare love, a savouring and a delighting and a melting away in love, and a constant renewal of all this. For there, where we are raised above reason and all our activities in naked vision, we are wrought by the spirit of our Lord. And there we suffer the inworking of God and are illumined by divine light, just as the air is illumined by the light of the sun and as iron is permeated by the strength and heat of fire. Thus we are transformed and penetrated from splendour to splendour, in the very image of the Holy Trinity . . . There the Father finds us and loves us in the Son, and the Son finds us and loves us with the same love in the Father. And the Father and the Son embrace us in the unity of the Holy Spirit, in a blessed delight which is eternally renewed, ceaselessly, in knowledge and in love, through the eternal birth of the Son from the Father and the outpouring of the Holy Spirit from them both.

The Seven Enclosures 172

The contemplative life: the simplicity of God

Now this active meeting and this loving embrace are in their ground blissful and modeless. For the fathomless being of God is so dark and so without particular form or manner that it contains all the ways of God, the activity and characteristics of the persons in the rich embrace of essential unity, thus creating a divine bliss in the abyss of the ineffable. Here there is a blissful crossing over and a self-transcending immersion into a state of essential bareness, where all the divine names and modes and all the living ideas which are reflected in the mirror of divine truth fall away into simple ineffability, without mode and without reason. For in this fathomless simplicity all things are contained in a state of blissful beatitude, while the ground itself remains completely uncomprehended, unless by essential unity. Here the Persons must yield, and all that lives in God, for here there is nothing but an eternal stillness in a blissful embrace of loving immersion.

This is that modeless essence which all fervent spirits have chosen above all things. This is that dark stillness in which all lovers lose their way. But if we could prepare ourselves in virtues, we would at once strip ourselves of our bodies and flow into the wild waves of the sea, from which no creature could ever draw us back.

The Spiritual Espousals 248

The *German Theology*

The author of this work (the *Theologia Deutsch* or the *Theologia Germanica*) is known to us only by the name of 'the man from Frankfurt'. We possess no details of his life, but it is believed that he belonged to the Knights of the Teutonic Order at Sachsenhausen, and that he came from Frankfurt am Main. This had originally been one of the military orders of the Church, a medieval phenomenon alien to us today whereby soldiers would combine their military profession with a religious vocation. The Teutonic Knights were created in 1190, during the Crusades, but by the late fourteenth century they were entirely involved in the colonization and administration of Central and Eastern Europe.

There has been some dispute about the dating of the *German Theology*, but the signs are that it is likely to have been written in the first part of the fifteenth century. Certainly its handling of the great Rhineland themes explored by Eckhart and Tauler is static: the author is transmitting and commenting on a tradition which is already formed and which he himself inherits, rather than creating anything new. It is also noticeable that of the full range of mystical themes developed by Eckhart and Tauler, it is the sublimation of our will into the will of God and the freeing of our mind from creatures to which the author gives main emphasis.

Even though the *German Theology* represents a stage in the development of the Rhineland school at which it has become to some extent detached from the soaring spiritual vision which inspired it, this work proved immensely popular and became one of the chief mediators of Rhineland spirituality to posterity. Its influence was particularly keen among the first generations of Protestant reformers. The reason for this is not least because the *German Theology* advocates an inward religion, which is personal and deeply felt, and it shows a natural antipathy towards all forms of ecclesiastic authority. This must have been one of its features which appealed to the young Luther, who originally discovered the work in 1515 and published it for the first time a year later. In his preface to a second, extended edition of 1518, Luther wrote that he had learned more from the *German Theology* than he had from any other book, with the exception solely of the Bible and St Augustine. Later reformers (but not Calvin) also held the book in high esteem; it stressed a simple, undogmatic faith, a passive acceptance of all manner of suffering and a resistance to the complexities of authority, which spoke in particular to the Pietists and Anabaptists in the turbulent centuries following the Protestant Reformation. In a later century, Charles Kingsley wrote warmly of the *German Theology*, contributing a preface to Susanne Wrinkworth's popular translation of the work (1874).

The translations are made from the new critical edition by W. Von Hinten, *Der Franckforter*, Munich 1982.

A glimpse of eternity

People ask if it is possible for the soul while still in the body to obtain a glimpse of eternity and thus to enjoy a foretaste of eternal life and eternal blessedness. Normally the answer to this question is that it is impossible, which is true for as long as the soul has its gaze fixed on the body and on the things which belong to the body, on time and on creatures, thus becoming filled with images and multiplicity: while this is so, such a thing cannot be. For if the soul wants to reach its goal, then it must become free of all images and creatures and, above all, free of itself.

Chapter 8

The true light and true knowledge

Let no one think that they shall come to this true light and true knowledge and to the life of Christ through much questioning, or by hearsay, or by reading and studying, or by great skill and mastery, or by high powers of natural reason. I say this: for as long as we lend importance to anything, do or use anything for our own pleasure, desire or ends, whether it be this or that, whether it be our very selves, or whatever it may be, for as long as we do this, we shall not attain these things.

Chapter 17

Our two eyes

Now the created soul of men and women has two eyes. The one possesses the power to see into eternity, while the other sees time and creatures, discriminating among them, and nourishes, orders and controls the body. But these two eyes of ours cannot both perform their work at the same time. But if the soul is to see into eternity with the right eye, then the left eye must cease to function and must behave as if it were dead. And if the left eye is to work in the external world, then the right eye must be hampered in its activity, which is contemplation. And so whoever wants the services of one eye must do without the other, for no one can serve two masters.

Chapter 7

Peace in suffering

There are no people living on this earth in undisturbed peace and calm, without troubles and frustrations, and for whom all things go according to their own will. Suffering here is inevitable, whatever we may do to avoid it. And the moment we are free of one difficulty, then two more take its place. Therefore we should willingly resign ourselves to the situation and seek only true peace of heart, which no one can take away, in order to overcome our distress: that peace, which breaks through all distress and frustration, all griefs, suffering, misery, disgrace and whatever else there may be, so that in the midst of all this we may be joyful and patient, as were the disciples and followers of Christ. Whoever now applies all their efforts with love to this task will soon know the eternal and true peace, which God himself is, according to their powers as a creature, so that what was formerly bitter will be sweet and their heart will remain steadfast in all things.

Chapter 12

God gives himself to all

Now when the Perfect One comes, we disdain all that is partial and imperfect. But when does he come? I say: he comes when he is known and sensed and enjoyed in the soul in as great a degree as is possible. The failure to come is entirely our fault and not his. It is just as when the sun illumines the earth and is as close to one person as it is to another, yet cannot be seen by a blind man. Then the problem is not in the sun but in the man who is blind. And in the same way that the sun cannot hide its light wherever the sky is free of cloud, but must illumine the earth, God, who is the highest good, does not wish to hide himself, wherever he finds someone in prayer, who is free of all creatures. For in so far as we empty ourselves of creatures, thus far we make ourselves receptive to God, neither more nor less. If my eye is to see something, then it must be free of all other things, and if heat and light are to enter, then cold and darkness must depart. This is how it must be.

Chapter 1

The life of Christ

Whoever knows and recognizes the life of Christ, knows and recognizes Christ. And, again, whoever does not know this life, does not know Christ. If we believe in Christ, then we believe that his life is the finest and most precious life that there has ever been and, if we do not, then we do not believe in Christ. In so far as the life of Christ is in us, thus far Christ exists within us, and if the one is not in us, then neither is the other.

Chapter 43

Love of the noble life

When someone lives in the true light and in true love, then this is the noblest, the finest and the most precious life which there ever was or ever shall be. This is why it must be loved and praised above all other forms of life. It exists in its greatest perfection in Christ, who would otherwise not be Christ. And the love for this noble life, and for all that is good, causes us to do and to suffer willingly and with dignity all that we are obliged to do and to suffer, however demanding for the natural man. Therefore Christ says: 'My yoke is easy and my burden is light' [Matt. 11.30]. This results from our love for this noble life. We can observe it in the apostles and the martyrs, who gladly suffered what they had to suffer and did not ask God that their suffering or their pain should be shorter or lighter or any the less, but asked only that they should remain firm and steadfast. Truly, all that belongs to divine love in the person who has become like God is so simple and right that it defies all description by mouth or by pen, except alone that it exists.

Chapter 41

Resting content with God

It is said: Those who rest content with God, need nothing more. And those who content themselves with something else, be it this or that, do not content themselves with God. But whoever contents themselves with God, will find no more contentment in anything else, but only in him who is neither this nor that but is all things. For God is the One and must be the One; he is all things and must be all things. And so whatever is but is not the One, is not God, and whatever is but is not all things and above all things, is not God. For God is the One and is above the One, and is all things and above all things.

Chapter 44

God the Father

Christ speaks further: 'No one can come to me unless the Father who sent me draws him' [John 6.44]. Now pay attention. By the Father I understand the one, perfect good, which is all things and above all things, without which there can be no true being, nor goodness and without which there could never be a single good work, either in the future or in the past. And since it is all things, then it must also be in all things and above all things. And it cannot be anything which the creature, as creature, can grasp and understand. For what the creature can grasp and understand as a creature corresponds to its creatureliness and must be something particular, this or that, and is thus also a created thing. But if the one, perfect good were something particular, if it were this or that, which the creature can understand, then it would not be all things and in all things and it would not then be perfect. This is why it is also called a nothingness. By this is meant that it is in no way something which the creature in its creatureliness can grasp, recognize, think or name. Now see, when this perfect, nameless one flows into a person who is about to give birth, then it gives birth in this person to its only begotten Son and, so doing, gives birth to itself in him. And so we call it Father.

Chapter 53

Two masters

In justice and in truth it ought to be the case that there is nothing in us which claims anything for itself, which desires, wills, covets or strives for anything other than God alone and what is his: that is the one, eternal and perfect good. But if this is not so for us, if we claim anything for ourselves, desire, will or strive for anything at all, for this or that or whatever it may be, more than we do for the perfect and eternal good, which is God himself, then this is to go too far and is a failing which will hinder us in our search for the perfect life. Thus we will never attain the perfect good, unless we take leave of everything, especially of ourselves. For no one can serve two masters, who are opposed to one another. If we want the one, then we must take leave of the other. And so, if the Creator is to enter, all creatures must depart.

Chapter 53

The *Book of Spiritual Poverty*

Unfortunately we know even less about the author of this work than we do of the Frankfurt man who wrote the *German Theology*. It similarly dates from the beginning of the fifteenth century, that is many years after the golden period of the Rhineland school, but was long thought to be the work of Johannes Tauler, under whose name it was published by the Protestant Daniel Sudermann in Frankfurt in 1621 (with the title *The Imitation of the Poor Life of Christ*). It was published again many times and a modern critical edition of the text appeared in 1877 by H. S. Denifle. It was Denifle also who in an acute introduction to his edition convincingly challenged the current attribution to Tauler, and suggested that the *Book of Spiritual Poverty* must have been the work of a Franciscan.

Like the *German Theology*, the *Book of Spiritual Poverty* evolved out of the Rhineland tradition, both transmitting it down the centuries and adding its own emphases. In general these could be described as a strong devotion to the passion of Christ, and a special feeling for the place of external poverty as a complement to an internal state of detachment. In a number of places the author calls explicitly for the embracing of external poverty (although in the text which we have translated here he shows a slightly more guarded attitude), and it is this combination of two of the great spiritual themes of fourteenth century life, poverty within and poverty without, which gives this book a special place in the history of Christian spirituality.

The critical text which serves as the basis for my translations is *Das Buch von geistlicher Armuth* by H. S. Denifle (Munich 1877), to which the page references given at the end of each passage refer.

What is spiritual poverty?

To have spiritual poverty is to become like God. But what is God? God is a being who is detached from all creatures. He is a free power and a pure act. Thus spiritual poverty is also a detachment from creatures. But what does detachment mean? That person is detached who clings to nothing. Spiritual poverty clings to nothing, and nothing clings to it.

p. 1

The voice of God I

The voice of the divine spirit within man is nothing other than the pure revelation of divine truth in which the human spirit is removed from its sensuality and is raised above all images and all faculties into the bareness of God's being. And there the spirit understands its own nobility and its nobility is so revealed that the spirit is united with the nobility of God and with his voice and with his spirit. As St Paul says: 'He who is united to the Lord becomes one spirit with him' [1 Cor. 17].

Now this being joined to God means nothing other than that the spirit goes out of itself according to its createdness and casts itself into a pure nothingness. And that nothingness is the divine image which has been imprinted in the soul and which remains there and cannot be destroyed. God takes that image and unites it with himself. And so the human spirit becomes one spirit with God through the divine image.

p. 44

The voice of God II

The spirit of God also speaks in the hearts of men and women. But he does not speak in images or in forms; rather he speaks in a way that is above both images and forms. And when he speaks, then for us it is life, light and truth.

p. 64

The voice of God III

The first way in which God speaks to us is in the essence of the soul, which no creature can penetrate nor in which any creature can speak, for God alone dwells there and he alone can speak there. And when God speaks there, the soul takes leave of all things, all its faculties fall silent and it glimpses the ground of its bare essence. And in this bareness and silence God speaks his word and the soul hears it. And this voice of God is nothing other than an inward sense of God within us, which springs forth from God into the essence of our soul and overflows all its faculties, causing such joy that we would gladly be free of all our own activity and allow God alone to work in the essence of our soul. And the more we leave our own activity, the more active God is in us.

p. 68

The work of God

God's work is nothing other than his revelation in the soul when he shows himself to the soul. Then God is both the one who does the work and the work itself. And he is what he works, and what he works he is. Therefore God draws the soul away from all things so that it can become receptive to his work. And God's work makes the soul one spirit with God, which is what God desires most from men and women, that they should allow him always to work within them without any obstruction, so that they may become one spirit with him.

p. 56

The Passion of Christ

Pagans too have sought the bare essence of the soul, but they could not gain entrance to it without Christ. And so they could not know God nor be blessed, although they certainly wanted to be so. This is how it is for those who seek the bare essence of their souls without the passion of Christ: such people shall never come to complete knowledge of the truth, which is God and which makes them blessed. For all our blessedness lies in Christ and in his passion. And therefore whoever wishes to attain true blessedness, must enter in through the passion of Christ. This is why our Lord says: 'It was necessary for Christ to suffer to come into the Kingdom of Heaven' [cf. Luke 24.46]. And it is through the passion of Christ that we too enter the kingdom of our souls, where we shall see God without intermediary. And so we shall arrive at our proper goal if we go by the way of his passion.

p. 63

The Holy Spirit

True divine love springs from the Father's heart when he utters his eternal word in the soul. And with this utterance the love of the Holy Spirit springs forth and overflows the soul and its faculties so that all that flows from the soul is itself love. And this causes the withdrawal of the senses into the inner man, the stilling of the soul's faculties and a great surge of love towards God. And so God is compelled to reveal himself in the soul and to utter his word, which is the source of all love.

p. 185

On dying in God

All things must die within us, as we must die in God. In this way we will produce much fruit, and bring forth the life which is most pleasing to God. And whoever do not enter within themselves, cannot inwardly die, and so shall not produce much fruit. The external appearance of poverty alone is not of great value – the street urchins have as much, and they are not holy. We should die inwardly then, in the ground of our soul, as well as pursue a life poor in goods, for these together are the poverty in which there is perfection.

p. 190

One love with God

The love of the Holy Spirit penetrates the whole of our body and inspires us with the fire of love. And so all the unlikeness to God that there is within us is consumed, and all that was twisted in us is made straight. And it seems to us that we are going to be burned up entirely by this love, which is called an active love. For as long as there remains any unlikeness in us, it has work to do, but when that work is done, then there arises within us a sweet form of love which is called a passive love, and which in still calm allows God to work in us. This love does not act, but it is God who acts, which this love allows him to do. And so the soul advances eternally into God, and God draws it on into himself and makes the soul one love with himself. Then it becomes one love with God and, if any name should be given it, that would be the name 'love' for then it contains nothing at all but love.

p. 193

Select Bibliography

GENERAL

Ancelet-Hustache, Jeanne, *Meister Eckhart and the Rhineland Mystics*. English tr., London, Longmans 1957.

Clark, J. M., *The Great German Mystics*. Oxford, Blackwell 1949.

Cognet, Louis, *Introduction aux mystiques rhéno-flamands*. Paris, Desclée 1968.

Davies, Oliver, *God Within: The Mystical Tradition of Northern Europe*. London, Darton, Longman & Todd 1988.

MEISTER ECKHART

Texts

Meister Eckhart, *Die Deutschen und Lateinischen Werke*, edited by the Deutschen Forschungsgemeinschaft. Stuttgart, Kohlhammer 1936ff.

Translations

Colledge, E. and McGinn, B., *Meister Eckhart: The Essential Sermons, Commentaries, Treatises and Defense*. Classics of Western Spirituality. New York, Paulist Press; London, SPCK 1981.

McGinn, B. with Tobin, F. and Borgstadt, E., *Meister Eckhart: Teacher and Preacher*. Classics of Western Spirituality. New York, Paulist Press; London, SPCK 1986.

Quint, Joseph, *Meister Eckhart, Deutsche Predigten und Traktate*. Modern German tr., Munich, Insel Verlag 1963.

Walshe, M. O'C., *Meister Eckhart: Sermons and Treatises*., 3 vols. London, Element Books 1987.

Studies

Smith, C., *The Way of Paradox*. London, Darton, Longman & Todd 1987.

Woods, R., *Eckhart's Way*. Delaware, Michael Glazier 1986; London, Darton, Longman & Todd 1987.

JOHANNES TAULER

Texts

Corin, A. L., *Sermons de J. Tauler et autres écrits mystiques. Ire. part, Le Codex Vindobonensis 2744; IIe part, Le Codex Vindobonensis 2739*. 2 vols, Paris 1924–9.

Vetter, F., *Die Predigten Taulers, aus der Engelberger und der Freiburger Handschrift, sowie aus Schmidts Abschriften der ehemaliger Strassburger Handschriften*. Berlin 1910.

Translations

Hofmann, G., *Johannes Tauler: Predigten*. Modern German tr., Freiburg, Johannes Verlag 1979.

Shrady, M., *Johannes Tauler: Sermons*. Classics of Western Spirituality. New York, Paulist Press; London, SPCK 1985.

JAN VAN RUUSBROEC

Texts

Alaerts, J. et al., *Jan van Ruusbroec: Opera Omnia*. Vols I, II. Leiden, E. J. Brill; Tielt, Lannoo 1981ff; vol. III in *Corpus Christianorum continuatio medievalis* C III, Turnhout, Brepols; Tielt, Lannoo 1988.

Poukens, J. B. et al., *Werken*. Mechelen-Amsterdam, 1932–4; 2nd edn Tielt 1944–8.

Translations

Colledge, E., *The Spiritual Espousals*. London, Faber and Faber 1952; Maryland, Westminster Press 1983.

Wiseman, J. A., *John Ruusbroec*. Classics of Western Spirituality. New York, Paulist Press; London, SPCK 1985.

Studies

Dupré, L., *The Common Life: The Origins of Trinitarian Mysticism and its Development by Jan Ruusbroec*. New York, Crossroad 1984.

Underhill, E., *Ruysbroeck*. London 1915.

Wautiers d'Aygalliers, A., *Ruysbroeck the Admirable*. English tr., London 1924.

THE *GERMAN THEOLOGY*

Texts

Von Hinten, W., *Der Franckforter*, Münchener Texte und Untersuchungen zur deutschen Literatur des Mittelalters. LXXVIII. Munich, Artemis Verlag 1982.

Translations
Hoffmann, B., *The Theologia Germanica of Martin Luther*. Classics of Western Spirituality. New York, Paulist Press; London, SPCK 1980.

THE *BOOK OF SPIRITUAL POVERTY*

Texts
Denifle, H. S., *Das Buch von geistlicher Armuth*. Munich 1877.

Translations
Kelley, C. F., *The Book of the Poor in Spirit*. London, Longman 1954.